Opéra et Boulevard des Capucines). — LL.

Colette

A taste for life

Colette

A taste for life

Yvonne Mitchell

Harcourt Brace Jovanovich

New York and London

Printed in Great Britain

ISBN 0–15–118513–1

First American edition

BCDE

Contents

SIDONIE-GABRIELLE COLETTE WAS BORN IN 1873 in a small village in Burgundy. She went to Paris at the age of twenty, where she unwillingly, but obediently, started her career as a writer at the instigation of her first husband.

Her books shocked the French bourgeoisie and, indeed, most of the critics; inspired thousands of adolescent boys and girls to write to her, identifying their thoughts and feelings with those of her characters; started a cult; and at the same time gained for her amongst other literary honours, the nomination of Chevalier of the Légion d'honneur on the same day as Marcel Proust.

For those who have never read her but know her name, she is vaguely associated with loose morals, with dancing in the nude in music-hall, with lesbian and homosexual circles, with divorce and lapsed Catholicism. In fact she was instinctively deeply moral, and although perhaps the most truly liberated woman of this century, she not only had no desire to shock but no wish to change anyone to her way of thinking or being. She lived through her five senses. She wrote of the earth with the sure touch of a biologist, of childhood with an impeccable sense-memory, of love with the instinct of a sensual woman. Though the quality of her writing was never in doubt, her choice of characters and milieux were thought by some of her contemporaries to be depraved. In *Chéri*, the love between a spoilt, irresponsible boy of eighteen and his ageing cocotte mistress was judged to be offensive, as was the love between a married woman and her husband's mistress in *Claudine en ménage*.

Colette herself had no belief in hierarchy, whether in love, society or on the 'tree of life'. She rated the life force pulsating anywhere, in a plant or an insect, as interesting and as worthy of her absorbed attention as the men she fell in love with or the child she bore; and she felt the love between two women or two men, or between a mother and child to be as worthy as the love between a man and a woman.

This one-time *enfant terrible* was acknowledged long before she died, just as she is today, to be among the great writers of modern times. She is the only Frenchwoman ever to have been given a state funeral.

Childhood

Childhood

S HE WAS BORN SO BLUE AND silent that the midwife and the servant present at the long and difficult confinement thought it useless to bother with her. They had also neglected to keep the fire alight in the chill room where her mother laboured for three days. But she survived in spite of them, and eight years later Sido, whose fourth child she was, confided in her usual unembarrassed and forthright manner: 'They say that children like you, carried so high, and who take so long to reach the light of day, are always the most beloved because they wanted to remain close to their mother and were so unwilling to leave her.' Though the attachment remained, the child savoured life with an independence much greater than that allowed most French children.

Colette has celebrated the incomparable years of her childhood in *Sido* and *La Maison de Claudine*; a childhood familiar with owls, lizards and caterpillars. In *Sido* she has paid homage to the solitude and freedom she enjoyed and which, when she had lost both, she sought with continual yearning. The freedom to contact, alone, with a feeling of privacy, almost of secrecy, the life teeming from the earth in the woods and forests round her native Burgundian village of Saint-Sauveur-en-Puisaye.

But she wrote of these times in the 1920s when she was nearly fifty. During her childhood and adolescence she felt no urge at all to express herself, in words or in any other medium. She simply lived with all her five senses, with an awareness informed by intelligence and love. To her the important thing was (and the excitement of it remained with her throughout her life) 'to lay bare and bring to light something that no human eye before mine has gazed upon', and like a dedicated naturalist she felt no need to show her discovery to others. The meeting, the response, was between her and what she uncovered. She never needed an onlooker, nor approbation; never saw herself looking, contemplating, listening, touching, smelling . . . felt no need to 'dim, by writing about it, my thrilling or tranquil perception of the living universe'.

PREVIOUS PAGE Minet-Chéri aged five.

When she did write about it, what she remembered was the reality rather than the fact, the intimacy rather than the broad outline: the cat Bijou suckling her chaplet of newborn infants whilst herself sucking, with an over-large tongue, at the teats of her old mother Nonoche – 'the purr-purr as of a log-fire ... the double purring, silver-toned and deep, that is the mysterious privilege of felines, that rumbling as of a distant factory, whirring of an imprisoned moth, windmill grinding to a halt'. Or she recalled a hidden spring which riffled over the grass like a snake, tasting of iron and hyacinth stalks; memories more vivid than on-the-spot reportage because distilled; as the scarlet geraniums and the foxgloves were distilled from all those summers, and as the winter sky lowering over the bare branches of the walnut tree and the female cats flattening their ears, were distilled from all those winters.

The freedom that Colette and her brothers and sister enjoyed was due to their mother's considered refusal to interfere in the daily life of her children. But this was an intellectual deliberation; paradoxically her instincts were above all motherly; and she was deeply informed with a sense of responsibility, so she would anxiously wait for their return on an autumn evening, peering up and down the street, her head or shoulders covered in whatever piece of clothing she had snatched up from the hall-stand in passing: a child's hooded cape, a blue apron, a man's overcoat. She would hurriedly withdraw before she thought she was seen, and the child Colette always kept up the pretence.

This mother – 'Sido', as Colette's father called her – had got her own love and understanding of the countryside and the plants and creatures that lived there from the same woods and forests where Colette made her first discoveries; but she was not a country woman by birth. She was born in Paris in 1835, of Henri-Marie Landoy, whom she referred to as 'the Gorilla' (he was one quarter negro) and Adèle-Sophie Chatenay, who died when Sido, the youngest of her children, was very small.

The child, Adèle-Eugénie-Sidonie, was sent to a peasant nurse on a farm a hundred miles from Paris, in a village bordering on Saint-Sauveur. Sido related to her youngest daughter snatches of this childhood, and how at the age of eight, she went back to live with the Gorilla and her much older brothers and sister, and a large monkey called Jean, in the house in Paris where her father manufactured chocolate.

She described to Colette how the slabs of chocolate would be laid out at night on the roof-terrace to dry. The child listening to her mother sometimes lost the thread of these stories, from pursuing in her own mind the vision of a parenthesis; of the soft slabs of

Sido.

chocolate showing every morning the 'imprints, like flowers with five hollow petals', of the paws of nocturnal cats.

Sido never lost touch with her nurse and the country farm; though the Gorilla remarried and went to Lyons, and Sido, at sixteen, left Paris to be with her brothers who were by then successful journalists in Brussels. Here she lived among the young intellectual French and Belgian artists, poets and musicians who were their friends. Her appreciation of these times is reflected in a letter she wrote to Colette in 1909, at the age of seventy-four, envying her daughter the pleasure of living with intelligent and cultured people: '. . . I have missed all this since the most beautiful years of my life, when my brother initiated me into the art of understanding and loving beautiful and rare things.' But again and again she returned to her nurse and the countryside of her childhood; and it was during one of these two-month-long visits in 1854, when she was nineteen years old, that she met Jules Robineau-Duclos, the gentleman proprietor of neighbouring farmland, known to the villagers and later to Sido herself, as 'the Savage'.

A French mother refers to her offspring with a mixture of pride and shame as *sauvage* not only if he is wild and untamed, but also if

Rue de l'Hospice, St-Sauveur-en-Puisaye – 'The front of the house, with its large graceless windows.' (*La Maison de Claudine*)

he enjoys solitude, or is merely unsociable enough not to wish to shake hands with visitors. Sido later referred lovingly to both her sons as *sauvages* because they escaped from the house at the first sign of callers, and because they returned from the woods dirty, scratched and with their clothes torn. Jules Robineau-Duclos rode alone on horseback, spent his evenings and a great part of his days drinking, and lived in a largish manor house in Saint-Sauveur, alone except for the numerous female servants he got with child. His well-to-do relations apparently decided it was time he had a legal heir to his properties, vineyards and farmlands, and set about, as French families have always done, arranging a marriage as a business transaction.

So Adèle-Eugénie-Sidonie Landoy came to live in the house with the good stables and the outbuildings where milk and cheese were produced, and where servants spun the flax grown on the estate into linen; the house where there was cut glass and family-engraved silver, but where the bedrooms were rough-cast and freezing cold, nearly bare and completely devoid of comfort. For his new wife's sake, the Savage tried to give up drinking, but after two months he came home one night and assaulted her violently; and instead of succumbing in wifely fashion and accepting her role, Adèle Eugénie-Sidonie, counter-attacked. She hurled everything that was on the mantelpiece at him, including a heavy candlestick which wounded him in the face, severely enough for him never to attempt to hit her again.

The encounter did not prevent either of them from growing more and more lonely. He continued to spend his days away from home; and she pined in the house where all the wifely accomplishments were performed by servants who resented her intrusion into their way of life. Though he never understood her, or what she wanted, he sometimes brought her presents to appease what he sensed was her unhappiness. Their first child, Juliette, was born after three years of marriage, and three years later she gave birth to a son, Achille, whom village gossips were quite certain was not his. Not long after the boy's birth, Jules died of drink and an apoplectic fit, lonely and un-attended, in a cold attic bedroom, leaving his wife proprietress of a good deal of farmland. In December of the same year, 1865, Sido married the local tax-collector, Jules-Joseph Colette; and that same house, that cold, lonely house, where nothing remained of Robineau-Duclos but the wrought iron initials of its railings, was transformed into the warm, loving home which Colette has immortalised.

The front of the house in the steeply sloping rue de l'Hospice retained its forbidding dignity, but the back, invisible from the street, became the centre of their family universe, the garden with

its twin firs and walnut-tree, its overgrown lawns and its hundred-year-old wisteria, its lilacs and its vine. In the stables a new young mare, in the coach-house a victoria draped in blue. Instead of the spinners of flax and the covey of pregnant maids; there was only one, Henriette, who arrived early morning, a washerwoman who came once a week, a sewing woman; and in the living room, mother dogs and their puppies, mother cats and their young. But upstairs, although a fire now burned in the grate, the big bedroom retained its chill. It was here that a son, Léopold, was born in 1868, and on 28 January 1873, a daughter, Sidonie-Gabrielle, blue and silent.

Colette and her brother Achille in the garden at St Sauveur. 'Ask me to tell you the shape and the colour of every leaf.' (*Paysages et portraits*)

'Minet-Chéri', as her mother called her, enjoyed many of the privileges of a youngest child. She was allowed to go with her mother in the victoria to shop in Auxerre; she was not sent to boarding-school like her elder sister and brothers, who came home in winter thin, with chilblains on their hands and feet, and in summer covered with fleas; instead, Minet-Chéri – or Gabrielle, as she was known outside the family – attended the village school, walking down the steep rue de l'Hospice in the summer term, swinging her long fair plaits under the big straw hat which hid the wide forehead she never liked and in her grown-up life always covered with a network of fringe; two tame swallows in her pocket, the Nanny-like bitch Toutouque at her heels. In the winter she walked between two high walls of snow in her stout wooden clogs, carrying the heavy metal box of live coals and ashes that each child took to school to keep her warm.

Her impression of the school, described in her first book, *Claudine à l'école*, is that of thousands of village schools all over France: black pinafores; desks worn down so low that the children crouch over them with humped backs; assembling in the asphalt playground at 7.30 in the morning for the summoning indoors at ten minutes to eight; the little girls' classroom, the boys' entrance; the inspectors; school-leaving exams; and – of all her senses Colette's sense of smell was the most highly developed – the stench of unwashed young villagers ranged in tight formation between shut windows and doors.

Against this background what is vividly individual in the book is the uncomplicated and yet fully alive description of the heroine's uninhibited animal egotism, her classmates' stupidity, her tall friend's preoccupation with eating chalk, blotting paper, rubbers, pen-ends, and the dialogue of their robust adolescence. It is evidently from school and not from her parents, neither of whom were by birth Burgundian, that Colette acquired the rolling Rs of her native accent.

Away from school on summer mornings, she begged Sido to wake her at half-past three so that she could set off, in these fresh early

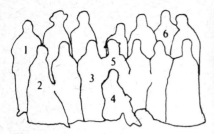

Family portrait: *1* Léo *2* Juliette *3* Sido
4 Minet-Chéri *5* Jules-Joseph Colette
6 Achille.

hours when she felt at one with the air, the first bird and the newly rising sun, for the bend in the river where the strawberries and blackcurrants grew. Unlike her mother who had learnt to curb her own curiosity if discovery meant the death of the flower or creature she was studying, Colette wanted to *feel* the fine dust on the wings of the moth, to unearth the chrysalis, to question the plant by tasting it. Maurice Goudeket, who was with her for the last thirty years of her life, has described in *Près de Colette* how in her sixties she had not lost these desires:

> She separated the petals of flowers, examined them, smelled them for a long time, crumpled the leaves, chewed them, licked the poisonous berries and the deadly mushrooms, pondering intensely over everything she had smelt and tasted. Insects received almost the same treatment; they were felt and listened to and questioned. She attracted flies and wasps, letting them alight on her hands and scratching their backs. 'They like that,' she would claim. When at last she left the garden she would pick up her scarf, hat, slippers, stockings, dog and husband, which she had shed one after the other. With her nose and her forehead covered with yellow pollen, her hair in disorder and full of twigs, a bump here and a scratch there, her face innocent of powder and her neck moist, stumbling along out of breath, she was just like a bacchante after libations.

Sido's attitude to nature was as practical as her attitude to religion. Although she never actively stopped her children from church practices, she had a devastating way of withering their zeal. Minet-Chéri at ten years old was naturally seduced by the smell of incense and the white roses surrounding the plaster Virgin on May Day. She came home full of pride to show her mother her 'blessed posy'. 'Sido laughed her irreverent laugh.... "Do you think it wasn't already blessed, before?"'

Sido's way of celebrating Christmas was not to attend the Midnight Mass, but to get up early and bake the traditional hundred loaves of bread for the poor of the village. Minet-Chéri, as the youngest child, had the privilege of offering the loaves and a ten-centime piece to each of the villagers who came. Her religious upbringing was so unconventional for a French Catholic child that many years later when the poet Francis Jammes sent her an advance copy of one of his books, she wrote in thanking him: 'You know I can't say very much about *L'Eglise habillée de feuilles* because I don't know anything about God....' As a child she was superstitiously attached to the seasonal festivals, to dates marked by a flower, a cake, a present. From instinct she 'ennobled with paganism the Christian fêtes', in love only with the branch of palm, the red Easter egg, the syringa, the aconite and the camomile flowers laid on the altar. 'I inhabited a paradise, dear harmless priest, that you could never have inspired; peopled with my gods, my talking animals, my nymphs and my satyrs ... and I listened to you talking about your hell, and thought what arrogance man has, that for his passing sins he invented the eternal Gehenna.'

Sido herself sometimes went to church, taking the hound Moffino with her, and quarrelled with the priest who objected to his barking at the elevation. But life to Sido was not prayer; it was the succouring of creatures and plants which but for her might die; it was opening her door to tramps or to stray animals. All creatures, her children included, were free to live how they chose without her intervention, but they were not free to die; not if she could save them. Not only was this passion for the life force pulsating around her shared by her daughter, but so too was the avoidance of its opposite: sickness and death. At ten years old, thinking that she might have to deliver some flowers from the garden to a neighbour who was ill, the child recoiled, snorting like an animal. She felt her mother's hand catch the end of one of her plaits: 'Be quiet! ... I know.... I'm the same ... but you must never say so.' Sido, who would send her all round the village to deliver choice bouquets of her favourite flowers, and who offered a ten-month-old baby boy one of her prized roses, refused quite harshly to sacrifice her flowers for a wreath. 'My moss roses, on a dead man! What a shocking thing to ask!' And Colette herself wrote many years later that the sufferings of love were 'no more to be revered than old age and illness, for both of which I am acquiring a great repulsion: both want to hold me close very soon. In advance I'm blocking my nostrils. ... The love-sick, the betrayed, the jealous, must smell the same odour.'

Sido did try to obey the outward convention of approaching old age like the rest of her generation when they were nearing fifty, but the children, individually, objected vociferously, and she was forced to put aside the frilled lace cap, and the black Sunday bonnet with its ruched ribbon and violets. Children who admit age even in their favourite animals will not accept the ageing of their mother, who must always remain for them as they first became consciously aware of her looks, probably around their sixth or seventh year.

From the love and understanding that existed between Colette and her mother it might seem that she was a favourite, if not an only child, but Colette herself believed that Achille was Sido's greatest pride and joy: 'Beauty' she called him, and described how when he was seven years old the Prussian soldiers had turned in the streets to look at him. 'You see they had never seen such wavy chestnut hair, such deep blue eyes, and especially such a mouth.' When he was twenty-two Sido was still admiring him in much the same terms. He had broken a window-pane to get into the house after having left his sister Juliette's wedding-party in disgust: 'Just think, he broke the glass because he wanted to be alone, far away from those sweating people, and to sleep caressed by the night wind. Was there ever such a wise child?' Yet she was only too aware of the dangers of mother-love. 'Madame Thorazeau is a harpy, an evil mother, an old horror, a dangerous fool ... she's carrying out an abominable blackmail to get her daughter back ... every time she looks at that wedding photo by her bedside she casts an evil spell. ... Well, that woman is teaching me everything a mother should take care *not* to do.'

Two of her four children, Colette and Achille, lived to the full in the world in which they found themselves, whilst retaining their independence of thought and behaviour. The other two could never adapt themselves to it, and lived each in his own, and totally different, world of fantasy.

The eldest child, Juliette, was even alien to the family circle. She was thirteen years older than Minet-Chéri, who as a schoolgirl of nine or ten years old would visit her on her school-free Thursday mornings, in the bedroom on the first floor, the bedroom with the cornflower wallpaper, the lace curtains lined with acid blue, the bedroom which later Colette proudly occupied.

Juliette spent the freedom her mother granted her, not in the woods where her brothers and young sister roamed, but lying in bed absorbed in reading: Stendhal, Victor Hugo, Oliver Goldsmith, classics, frivolous novels or magazine stories. Her head was so full of literary romances that she neither saw nor heard what went on around her. Minet-Chéri would visit her out of curiosity, envy of the pastels and silks for embroidery which tumbled out of the cupboard, and a feeling of high-minded boredom.

Thin, anaemic-looking, with the high cheek bones and slanting black eyes of a Tibetan girl, Juliette was totally sapped of energy by the thick tent of coarse, weighty hair that reached to her feet, that her mother daily brushed and braided and arranged in hideous fashion around the pale face. Sido, for all her independence of conventions, never dreamed of cutting it; it was a misfortune and it had to be borne.

Surprisingly, Juliette at twenty-five married a young doctor from the same village and went to live in the house on the other side of the rue de l'Hospice, whose shuttered windows could be seen from the cornflower bedroom. This was at the time, when Colette was twelve, that the family fortunes were dwindling disastrously, and Jules-Joseph Colette found himself, immediately after his step-daughter's marriage, unable to carry out the financial obligations involved in the transaction. In retaliation Dr Roché and his parents forbade Juliette ever to speak to or acknowledge her family again.

In the village agog with eager gossip, Sido was distraught with misery at the plight of her unhappy child, and Juliette herself took an overdose of pills, but at this first attempt, failed to die. Some months later, rumour reached the family that Juliette was big with child. Minet-Chéri, looking out of her window on a night of full moon, heard the first long-drawn-out cry of her stepsister in labour, and saw the small figure of her mother in a white dressing-gown cross the road to the garden opposite which bordered on the house with the closed shutters. She saw her 'press upon her own loins with both hands, spin round and stamp upon the ground as she began to assist, to reflect with her low groans, with the rocking of her tormented body and the clasping of her helpless arms, with all the pangs and the strength of motherhood, the pangs and the strength of the wretched daughter, who, out of reach, was giving birth to a child'.

Colette herself knew this oneness of identification, it permeated her everyday life. She identified not only with human beings but with animals, insects and plants. All nature was to her on the same level of the tree of life, and each manifestation of the life force as important and as capable of being understood by her as her own species. Her relationship with an individual insect was as vivid in her memory after thirty-three years as any childhood link with another human being.

'Minet-Chéri, come and see if my caterpillar has gone to sleep. I believe she's going to become a chrysalis and I've put a small box of dry sand down for her. She's an emperor-moth. I think a bird must have pecked at her stomach but she's recovered....' The caterpillar was, perhaps, asleep, moulded to the curve of a branch of box-thorn. The devastation around her attested to her strength: shreds of leaves, bitten stalks, denuded tree-shoots. Plump, thick as my thumb, more than a centimetre long, she puffed out the cabbage-green tyres of her body, spotted with turquoise hairy studs. I detached her and she wriggled, angry, showing her paler belly and all the little spiked legs which clung like suckers to the branch as I put her back. . . .

'Maman, she's eaten everything!' . . . I can see it all still before my eyes, the garden with its warm walls, the last dark cherries hanging from the tree, the sky fingered with long pink clouds. . . . Everything is there to my touch: the vigorous revolt of the caterpillar, the thick, damp, leathery leaves of the hydrangea – and my mother's hardened little hand.

As for her cats and dogs, she would always participate in what they felt, and Maurice Goudeket writes in *Près de Colette* that she would say to Souci, her French bulldog bitch, who was given to lying, 'I hear what you're thinking!', and the checked animal would lower its head in shame.

She describes her childhood self in *Les Vrilles de la vigne* in which she says to Claudine, 'You cannot imagine what a queen of the earth I was when I was twelve! Strong, rough-voiced, with two tightly-plaited pigtails whistling around me like whiplashes, reddened scratched hands, marked with scars, a square, boyish forehead.... Ah! How you would have loved me when I was twelve, and how I miss me!' But she seems not to have changed during the next few years, either physically or in her tastes; and the miracle of childhood continued for her.

She was not considered anything but an averagely good pupil, perhaps because her understanding had no need of expression, or perhaps because her teachers were unqualified to judge. Certainly, when she was eleven or twelve years old, she gained a very poor mark for an essay on Autumn, when the children were asked to write about their favourite season, and all the others, as was expected of them, chose to write about Spring. Above her essay the teacher, with all the superiority of an adult, had written: 'Shows imagination, but one senses a deliberate attempt to appear original.'

However when, at sixteen, with the rest of her class and teacher she went to Auxerre to sit for the school-leaving exam, she obtained her *brevet élémentaire*. It had no academic value but it marked the end of her childhood; and with the speed at which Paradise can be lost, within a year she and her whole family had been obliged to leave their beloved home in Saint-Sauveur.

During the five years since Juliette's marriage, family affairs had grown gradually worse. One by one the farms and farmland had been sold to pay off the tenant farmers from whom Jules-Joseph had borrowed money. In his desire to do better for his beloved Sido he had invested her money badly and by the time his younger daughter was seventeen, the family was financially ruined and the house and furniture had to be sold at public auction.

Jules-Joseph Colette was born in Toulon in 1829, and as a young man had entered the military academy at Saint-Cyr. He was made a Captain at the age of twenty-six, but his thigh was shattered three years later at the battle of Marignan, and his leg had to be amputated. As compensation he was given the red ribbon of the Légion d'honneur and some years later the appointment by the Ministry of Finance as tax-collector in the small village of Saint-Sauveur, a district and occupation far removed from his interests. Gregarious, he found it difficult to settle down to the small life of a village street and was completely out of his element in the countryside that so absorbed his family. Apart from army affairs his chief interest was in politics; he read avidly, not only books, but serious newspapers, reviews, science magazines and was a member and active correspon-

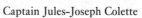

Captain Jules-Joseph Colette

dent of the Société de géographie. Gradually his interests diminished to become totally centred round his adored Sido whom he was forced to share with the demanding children, animals and plants that daily occupied her.

In *Sido* Colette remembers him writing passages of rhetorical prose, and odes with 'gorgeous rhythms, sonorous as a mountain storm', but his life as a writer was chiefly confined to the setting out of a writer's materials on his worktable: pads of blotting paper, pens with different nibs, a bronze inkpot, sealing-wax, glue, reams of white paper. After his death, Achille found a dozen volumes in cardboard bindings with black linen spines, with such titles as *My Campaigns, Marshal McMahon as seen by one of his companions-in-arms, Elegant Algebra*, etc. Each volume contained two or three hundred pages of white paper, entirely blank, except for the one dedicatory page at the beginning 'To My Dear Soul, her faithful husband, Jules-Joseph Colette'.

As a child Colette scarcely noticed her father. Only later did she think about him, recollect, and deeply regret that she had not understood his warm and loving character. Her preoccupation inside her home was with the forever suckling cats and bitches and their off-spring. There were few grown-up male animals, and she could not help noticing that Sido dealt shortly with them. When Moffino, the hunting dog, sat beside a basket of his newborn puppies Sido shooed him away. Minet-Chéri wept: 'Poor Moffino, where can he go?' 'To wherever his role as a father takes him,' replied her mother. 'To the tavern, or to play cards with Landre, or to flirt with the washer-woman.'

Jules-Joseph, adoring his wife as he did, must often have felt disparaged in a world where not only the females, but his young sons, and even the male dogs, ignored him.

'Go on, UP!', my father ordered Moffino in his beautiful Captain's voice.
But the dog, standing by the carriage step, wagged his tail coldly and looked towards my mother.
'Get up, animal,' my father repeated. 'What are you waiting for?'
'I'm waiting for the order,' the dog seemed to say.
'Allez, jump!' I called out, and I didn't need to say it twice.
'Very odd,' observed my mother.
'It only goes to show how stupid the animal is,' my father replied.

But even at ten years old Colette sensed his humiliation.

Colette noted towards the end of her life, in *L'Etoile Vesper*, that the male characters in her early books – Renaud, whom Claudine marries, Maxime in *La Vagabonde*, and Jean in *L'Entrave* – 'scarcely rise above the level of a male extra'.

It was not until 1921 with Chéri, and two years later with Phil in *Le Blé en herbe* that she created male characters as subtle and as alive as their women. And both Chéri and Phil were very young. The reactions of the two young males of the Colette household, Achille and Léo, to a mother-centred universe, were as different as Minet-Chéri's were from Juliette's, though the two boys spent a great deal of time in each other's company, and never quarrelled. Achille, though like his brother and sisters totally ungregarious (he would escape through a window at the first sign of callers, and hide up a tree with his book), was nevertheless seriously determined to be a doctor. As a very young man, obeying the same instincts as his mother's for any young creature in distress, he had smuggled home from the county town barracks where he was a volunteer, a piglet-like little bulldog bitch, Toutouque, who with all the other barrack dogs had by an idiotic order been condemned to death. Toutouque would lie on her back, ecstatic with love, whilst Achille pinched each of her teats in turn, to the tune of Boccherini's *Minuet*.

Léo aged thirteen. 'He was as gentle as could be and utterly unmanageable.' (*La Maison de Claudine*)

Léo, five years Achille's junior, was slight, dark, elfin and elusive, and remained the same into old age. As a small child he was continually disappearing, to be found in a clock tower in a neighbouring town, in the ivy-mantled Saracen Tower at Saint-Sauveur, or in a village churchyard fifteen miles away. He made cardboard tombstones for imaginary people, for whom he wrote epitaphs. At six years old he followed a one-eyed travelling clarinettist for three miles, and on his return, after waiting patiently while his anxious mother scolded him – she had had all the wells in the neighbourhood searched – he sat down at the piano and played all the clarinettist's airs, accompanying them with simple harmonies. He could do the same with the melody of a once-heard symphony. Colette also had this musical ability, which they had both inherited from their father. At a gathering after the first performance in Paris of Rimsky-Korsakov's *Scheherazade* in 1893, not long after Colette's marriage, Debussy was trying excitedly to recapture the pizzicato of the double bass, and Colette was able to hum and pick it out for him on the piano. 'Good memory!' he cried to her, 'good memory!' 'As if he were saying "Good news! Good morning!"' In those days music was more natural to her than writing; even later she often heard the rhythm of a sentence before the words.

But though Sido was convinced that young Léo would make a career in music, he wanted nothing better than to remain a child. And he partly succeeded. When he grew up he took the least demanding clerk's job he could find which would leave him free to dream or to compose music in his head. He scarcely bothered to eat, or to dress properly. In his sixties, he would occasionally visit Colette in

her apartment in the Palais-Royal, to open and silently examine her watch. Whenever anyone with a car would take him, he returned to Saint-Sauveur to climb the Saracen Tower and visit the haunts of his childhood, agonised if a new generation had changed an exact scene he remembered, or if a gate no longer creaked on the same four notes as it had fifty years before.

'I was fourteen or fifteen, with long arms, straight back, too small a chin, and clear blue eyes.' (*La Maison de Claudine*)

At the time of the family ruin, Colette was the only one still living at home. Léo had begun a brief period of studying pharmacy in Paris. Achille was by this time married and already a dedicated and overworked country doctor; he nevertheless made himself responsible for his parents and young sister and bought a small house for them in the village where he practised: Châtillon-sur-Loing (known today as Châtillon-Coligny).

Colette was seventeen. The house in the Loiret although poor and small, was nevertheless full of cats and dogs; there was a garden where mint and lilacs grew, and where Sido trained a climbing vine; there were tomatoes and seedlings under glass frames.

Colette accompanied her brother on his rounds, getting out of the two-wheeled carriage to walk up the steep hills so as not to overtire the mare, waiting outside while he paid his visits, reading her book, eating her snack of bread and redcurrant jelly, and plucking grass and green oats for the mare. The two plaits were now braided into one, though the wide ribbon *à la Vigée-Lebrun* was still tied around her forehead. Her skirts had been lengthened two years before.

Life had not changed a great deal for her father either. He still read *La Revue bleue* and *La Revue des deux mondes* and corresponded with his former classmate and publisher of scientific books, Albert Gauthier-Villars. By one of those tiny unimportant chances that are sometimes the precursors of great events which we cannot imagine *not* having happened, the thirty-five-year-old son of this publisher came to visit a friend in the Loiret district, and called upon his father's acquaintance. Henry Gauthier-Villars (known as 'Willy') was stout, balding, and wore opulent blond moustaches with narrowed points. A journalist and writer on a great variety of subjects, he was very much part of the Parisian scene of the 1890s. Colette formed a romantic admiration for him and on his part he wrote to his friend Marcel Schwob that he was 'completely bowled over by the airy grace of my pretty little Colette'.* Nevertheless they had a two-year long engagement during which time he visited the family very seldom 'bringing books, magazines, sweets, and then leaving. The great event in our engagement as far as I was concerned was our correspondence, the letters I received and the letters I freely wrote.'

They were married in Châtillon-sur-Loing on 15 May 1893. It was a quiet wedding, witnessed only by the family, the local timber

M. Willy 'His mouth under the dyed grey-gold moustache was narrow, dainty, and had something faintly English about its smile.' (*Mes apprentissages*)

* 'Colette' can be a Christian name or a surname in France.

merchant and his wife, and two of the bridegroom's friends from Paris, Pierre Véber and Adolphe Houdard. The bride wore simple muslin instead of the usual slipper-satin, and an everyday ribbon round her hair instead of wax flowers. Sido, flushed as always when she was unhappy, avoided her all day. Not only had her own first marriage been a terrible shock to her, but since the disaster of Juliette's marriage, she had been haunted by the irrational fear that her younger daughter might be abducted. On the first night that Minet-Chéri had moved to the cornflower bedroom, Sido had been unable to sleep because she was out of her hearing and had carried the sleeping child back to the little 'porter's' room which adjoined her own. Four years later when the fifteen-year-old girl was staying as a paying guest with girls of her own age for the holidays, Sido had a violent maternal vision of abduction and had taken a train-ride abruptly to bring her daughter back from the unoffending family. Now, at the wedding, she had nothing but memory and intuition to judge by, but they were enough to make her unhappy.

The bride herself unwittingly added to Sido's apprehension. She wandered in from the garden, pinning a bunch of dark red wild carnations to her dress, and at the wedding supper between the sea-pike with sauce mousseline and the sweet course of *bastions de Savoie*, fell asleep. She woke to hear her husband's voice: 'She looks a bit like Beatrice Cenci'; and Pierre Véber adding: 'With those red carnations she looks more like a dove with a dagger in its breast'; then Sido's aggressive reply: 'Can't you find anything better to compare her with than a decapitated woman and a wounded bird?'

'Next day I felt separated from that evening by a thousand leagues, abysses, discoveries, irremediable metamorphoses.'

Willy

PREVIOUS PAGE 'The window ... where I spent most of my time waiting and listening.' (*Chambre d'hôtel*)

Willy '... an already ageing man with bluish eyes, an impenetrable glance, and a terrifying gift for tears'.
(*Mes apprentissages*)

SHE TRAVELLED BY TRAIN WITH HER husband and his two friends to Paris. Paris, where the first motor-cars were still out-numbered by the horse-drawn carriages in the Champs-Elysées, where music-hall was very much in vogue with its risqué songs and suggestive sketches; the Paris of Toulouse-Lautrec, of Emile Zola and the recently built Eiffel tower, left-over from the Great Exhibition.

This was the time, as André Rouveyre wrote, of childish and inconsequent performances. You could watch Tiarko Richepin jumping on the piano with his feet tied together to show how original his music was, or you could listen to Sacha Guitry giving lectures with his mouth full of sandwiches.

As introduction to Paris Willy took his country wife to his bachelor digs at the top of a house on one of the Quais; a room filthy with thick lumps of dust mingled with matted hair that were blown under the large bed by the draughts which whistled under the door; a room he specifically did not want cleared up, full of trunks and portfolios containing pornography, piles of yellowing newspapers, and everywhere German 'dirty' postcards 'glorifying ribboned knickers, socks, and bare thighs'. Willy had been born into a highly respectable, religious and conventional family, and at thirty-five had apparently not outgrown the need to overthrow totally his restrictive upbringing. It was also fashionable in Paris in the Nineties for the better-off intellectuals to go slumming. Painters' studios were rented not by poor painters but by the 'Bohemian' society who emulated their *modus vivendi* and their décor.

Willy had the reputation of being irresistibly seductive, though the photographs, paintings and caricatures of the time do not give an inkling of why.

'M. Willy was not huge, he was bulbous,' Colette wrote in *Mes apprentissages*, '... it has been said that he bore a marked resemblance to Edward VII. To use a less flattering, but no less august comparison, I would say that in fact the likeness was to Queen Victoria.'

He was paunchy and balding, thick-necked and short-legged. But Colette also said that he had an impenetrable glance and a marvellously husky voice, which were possibly responsible for his charm. Some of his conquests probably came from the Bohemian background he wished to adopt, and those with backgrounds similar to his own perhaps shared his nostalgia for the city dirt they had been denied in their upbringing. That he should be captivated by Colette to the point of marrying her seems strange; though with her background of Châtillon-sur-Loing it would have been almost impossible to seduce her and he could not have imagined that either the Captain or Sido would have allowed her to go to Paris with him as a single girl.

She was obviously an entirely new attraction, utterly different from any girl or woman he could have met either with his family or in his Paris philanderings; and apart from his ever-present wish to surprise and shock he must also have found it irresistible to play Pygmalion. The girl was not only ignorant of men, she was ignorant of the world as he knew it. And for a man who 'preferred socks to stockings', as he later wrote of himself under a pseudonym, she was deliciously young – that is, at the time of the engagement. That he should have kept up the engagement for two years before marrying her, without seemingly giving either her or her parents any explanation, is not altogether puzzling, since his fear of commitment was as great as his love of doing the unexpected, and playing social games was one of his chief joys. By playing games with Colette and her family, keeping them waiting without any reason, he made himself from the outset the decider and the master.

It is more apparent, in this seemingly incongruous match, why Colette should fall for the older, more worldly man. His proposal was both exciting and flattering; added to which it had the blessing of her parents (Sido, for all her fears, could not have objected to the suitor's background). In spite of her deep-rooted love of the country, her home and her mother, Colette both dreaded and longed to be initiated into the mysteries of sex, both feared to lose her independence and wanted to share her life with the man she loved; and answered, as most girls do, with that thrill that is a mixture of panic and eagerness, the call of her future as a wife. Yet she already sensed diminution at becoming after all 'only a woman', at losing the 'secret certainty of being a precious child, of feeling inside myself the extraordinary soul of an intelligent man and a loving woman', that 'soul fit to burst my little body'. To be relegated to the role of a mere female is one thing, but Colette also feared being classified as an individual of one species. What she had dreamed, and indeed lived as a child, was a one-ness with the universe. She felt diminished and shrunken by the knowledge that she was now being weaned away from the whole to become only a fragmented part. Babies do not distinguish between themselves and an outward otherness, they are a part of their mother, the sky, their family pet. The first step towards individuality is the learning of words to distinguish one thing from another, and themselves from everything else. Even at three years old a child can be disturbed by a stranger picking him out from his surroundings by drawing attention to himself as a separate entity. What Colette, as late as seventeen, dreaded was tearing herself away from this whole and becoming identified as 'Willy's wife'.

This did not happen to her. She kept the link with 'tree, flower, timorous and gentle animal, the secret water of untapped springs', as she confessed fifteen years later to her alter ego, Claudine, in 'Le Miroir', one of the short stories in *Les Vrilles de la vigne*.

There was also, at seventeen, another, more usual fear. In those days no girl was forewarned by her mother, except in veiled hints, of what marriage entailed, and the step was a blind and daring dive into the deep. The shock of the initiation, far removed from their romantic fears of anticipation, changed young girls overnight, as Colette wrote, 'irremediably'.

As to being a housewife, her un-preparedness mattered not at all; apart from breakfasts of croissants and hot chocolate eaten in a dairy on the other side of the bridge, she lived on sweets.

She did not have to suffer the filthy room for long however; very soon they moved to a sunless, three-roomed apartment on the third floor of a house in the rue Jacob, where the previous occupant had maniacally covered the doors, cornices and walls with miniscule pieces of coloured confetti. Colette now had the comfort of an angora cat, loved by her and by Willy, whom they called Kiki-la-Doucette, which was also one of Willy's pet-names. With Kiki she stayed in the dark apartment all day, afraid to go out alone in Paris, writing daily letters to Sido which lied about her existence, whilst Willy went about those nefarious activities which at first she only dimly apprehended. It was in the evening that their life together began, when he initiated her into a number of varied social and pro-fessional activities.

Willy was the highly successful and widely read music critic of *L'Echo de Paris*, and in this capacity attended all the concerts given in Paris. He also liked to be seen at the theatre, and took a delight in music-hall. From the portraits, photographs and diary-type writings of the time as well as from her own descriptions of herself, it seems that Colette, paraded by her husband, gave the impression of a fox on a chain. Cocteau remembers her at the skating-rink, 'a thin, thin Colette, a sort of little fox dressed up for cycling, a fox-terrier in

skirts, with a black patch of hair over one eye, drawn up to her forehead with a bow of red ribbon'.

Late at night the 'thin, thin Colette' would wait, dropping with
fatigue in an outer office of *L'Echo de Paris*, whilst Willy fastidiously
corrected his copy. Then, finishing in the early hours of the morning, he would take her for a drink, sometimes to La Brasserie
Gambrinus where heavy, bearded men bet on the amount of beer
they could swallow in an atmosphere of thick smoke and Gothic
beams, or sometimes to the café D'Harcourt in the Latin quarter
which Colette preferred because they sat at a table with very young
men of Willy's acquaintance. She would sit quietly drinking lemon-
ade, whilst equally young prostitutes, ignoring her, treated the
young men with impartiality.

In contrast to these activities, Willy sometimes took her into the
private Salons where the cream of intellectual society gathered, the
very heart of Paris of la Belle Epoque. Willy of course, as a brilliant
music critic, was welcome at both the musical and the literary
gatherings. Colette might have been envied the famous people she
met at these soirées, but to her they were just people, and she a
gauche outsider. Madame Arman de Caillavet, the peremptory-
voiced and celebrated mistress of Anatole France – then the doyen of
French literature – entertained in her Salon, among her chosen
friends, the poets Catulle Mendès, Pierre Loüys and Paul Valéry,
and also – although he irritated his hostess with his effeminate
gentleness – the then twenty-two-year-old Marcel Proust.

Proust came one evening to the avenue Hoche with a companion
scarcely older than he, and like him graceful and a whisperer. They came
together and left together walking in step. Behind them the storm ex-
ploded. Madame Arman de Caillavet burst out: 'Oh no! It's not possible!
Did you see? The tender-twins behaviour! Those love-bird manners!
Really that child goes too far! Advertising ... as if the intention to shock
makes it less ridiculous. What have you to say Monsieur France? I ask
you, really ... well Monsieur France! I'm talking to you! What's the
matter with you?' Our unanimous silence warned her at last, and she
turned round. Behind her Marcel Proust was leaning against the jamb of
the door he had opened, the delicate colour gone from his cheeks and lips.
'I had.... I wanted to take ...', he stammered. 'What? What? You
wanted what?' barked Mme de Caillavet. 'A book that Schwob gave me.
... I left there ... on the sofa ... I'm sorry ...' He found the strength to
take the book and to escape. The following silence was not pleasant for
any of us. But our valorous hostess just shrugged her strong bare shoulders
adorned with diamonds. 'Oh, well ... what does it matter? ...'

At the 'musical Fridays' of Madame de Saint-Marceaux Colette
met Claude Debussy, Maurice Ravel and César Franck. Unsociable
though she may have been and ignorant at the time of the people

around her, she later recalled her first impression of them with absolute clarity. After that evening when they had heard *Scheherazade* for the first time, she remembers Debussy:

'Yes, yes, and the cellos go "mm-mm" in the base, and the timbals, my god the timbals, just a shudder which announces the explosion of the brass ...' With his mouth shut he miaowed in imitation of the violins ... he hammered on the rosewood piano with the poker, with his free hand he made a 'zzziii' down the length of the window, then clapped his lips together drily for the xylophone, and sang 'dong, dong' in a crystalline voice. Standing up, he used his voice, his arms and his feet; and two black locks of his hair spiralled over his forehead. His faun's laugh was not in response to our laughter, but in answer to something inside himself, and engraved on my mind was the image of the great master of French music, in the process of inventing, before our eyes, the jazz-band.

Ravel at that time made a totally different impression on her, scarcely an impression at all, though she was fascinated by his music. 'He had a distant manner,' she wrote, 'and a dry tone of voice.'

At Jeanne Muhlfeld's she met the new generation of writers: André Gide, Jean Cocteau, who much later became a great friend, and François Mauriac. 'I knew the yellow drawing-room,' Cocteau wrote, 'where Madame Muhlfeld played the game of chess which consists of making a writer immortal by moving him from square to square and finally placing him under a cocked hat and the dome of the Académie Française.'

At the *Temple d'Amitié* of the American Natalie Clifford-Barney there were the poetesses Lucie Delarue-Mardrus and Renée Vivien (born Pauline Tarn of a Scottish father and a Hawaiian mother), who translated Sappho, lived on alcohol and drugs, and died aged thirty-one in a stifling atmosphere of incense.

Most important to Colette's future were the Tuesdays of Rachilde, the perceptive literary critic of the *Mercure de France*.

Willy's wife must have seemed an oddity among all this brilliance; a country girl who rolled her Rs in a broad Burgundian accent, wore her hair, which stretched down her back as far as her calves, in one thick schoolgirl plait, and shied gauchely rather than shake hands.

Colette herself who, with her brothers, had run away to hide up a tree at the first sign of callers in Saint-Sauveur, found the contrast unnerving; as were the daytimes spent alone in the room with the slow-burning Salamander stove alight from September to June in the dark apartment in the rue Jacob, where she now lived not only on sweets but on nuts and bananas, tasting the difference between her one-time beloved solitude and her present fearful loneliness; between love and the 'laborious, exhausting sexual pastime'. 'I was just as miserable,' she later wrote, 'staying alone and forgotten in the

'Of all forms of absurd courage, the courage of girls is outstanding, otherwise there'd be fewer marriages.' (*Mes apprentissages*)

gloomy apartment, as finding myself obliged to go out.'

Her country girl's energy was sapped; mental shocks, loneliness, lack of food and the fumes from the stove all combined to lower her resistance. Added to which there were her social difficulties and her nightly jaunts. Whether she already suspected Willy's numerous infidelities (she wrote much later of herself at this period, 'No sooner married than deceived') is not clear. But she was gradually becoming aware, with a sense of nausea, of another, and more insidious practice: that of hiring, for the most minimal payment, a host of young talents to write the books and articles he signed with his own name. She found out only very gradually how Willy carried on this extraordinary 'editorship' and she has explained it in *Mes apprentissages*. He would write to one of his 'ghosts', say Curnonsky (later the famous gastronome): '. . . enclosed is a tiny sweet idea: throw upon this larva your connoisseur's eye and in fifty pages outline a future for it. . . .' The fifty pages would come back and be typed to wipe out any trace of another's hand, be put in a fresh envelope and sent to another 'ghost'. 'Help! Here is my newborn child. Can you, in one month, draw from it the rudiments of a light novel; milieu: a small Northern beach, half-wet bathing costumes . . . casino . . . young girls with sturdy calves . . . etc.' When the prescribed chapters were returned the manuscript was typed a second time and sent with a letter to a third therapeutist: 'Dear friend, no, it won't get going. A state of extraordinary prostration, extraordinarily unmerited . . . migraines . . . you want to know where I am with my next book? Here it is, isn't it enough to make you bang your head against the wall? Only your able good graces, that lightness of touch, that happiness of expression which I bow down to without envy, would be capable of transfusing this poor child with rich and joyous blood . . . it goes without saying that I shall know how to repay you. . . .'

As to his brilliant music criticisms which were so widely read that the sales of *L'Echo de Paris* rose by 50,000 copies when they appeared, the story is told by Sylvain Bonmariage in *Willy, Colette, et moi*. Bonmariage was a close friend and admirer of Willy, whose part he vehemently took against Colette when later public disputes arose about her own authorship. In praising him, Bonmariage cites that Willy, who had the reputation of being the maestro of the Wagnerian movement in France, and also of bringing to the public notice all the new composers, Dukas, César Franck, Fabre, Vincent d'Indy, Debussy, was given all his information in the way of taste and of technique by a 'boring' musician of great perception, Pierre de Bréville. De Bréville knew; Willy had the 'know-how'. Bonmariage rates the latter higher than the former. 'Willy could make or break a work,' he writes, and adds admiringly that Willy confided in

him that he had not written one word of his much-praised scientific book on colour photography. It had been bought by him from 'some poor wretch' for 500 francs (50 francs in today's currency). Willy, as he explained to his friend, had needed to impress his high-minded publisher father, who would not give him any money, of his seriousness as a writer. He succeeded, and the firm of Gauthier-Villars later published five other serious works 'by' Willy, including *L'Eclairage des portraits* and in another, just as serious vein, *Le Mariage de Louis XV* which was, in fact, written by a schoolmistress at the Ecole de Sèvres. 'But what does it matter?' writes Bonmariage, 'the end is achieved, Willy can cut the figure of an historian in the world of jokers, and that of a joker in front of historians.'

Perhaps Willy was not the only person to ply his strange trade, nor were his ghost-writers the only ones to ply theirs. In 'Le Képi' Colette recounts a story told her by Paul Masson of a woman who earned one sou a line. '"One sou!" I cried, "why only one sou?" "Because she works for a fellow who gets two sous a line, who works for a fellow who gets four sous a line, who works for a fellow who gets ten sous a line."' The story may have been Colette's own invention, or one of Paul Masson's jokes, but borrowers of other people's talent were certainly thriving as were publicity-mongers, hoaxers, punsters and pasticheurs. Everyone who was 'anyone' – and in this context Willy, maker and breaker of talents, was very definitely 'someone' – sought to amuse or better still to scandalise his confrères. Paris beneath – or rather above – the seriousness of her real artists and poets, was still living in that period of artificial stimuli which only the 1914 war would shatter. The *grandes cocottes*, whether kept in the sagging lap of luxury by a male lover or by the sharer of their sapphic idylls, wrote their memoirs in an atmosphere of stifling weightiness. In *Mes apprentissages* Colette describes the homes of these 'Lianes, Lines, Maudes, Vovonnes and Suzies', where heavy Louis XV furniture was draped with embroidered Japanese peacocks, where brocade and damask hung from walls and canopies, and so-called Arab boudoirs were windowless. The aim was to be exotic, but taste was not confined to one culture; the Japanese draperies shared the salons with lion-skins and live monkeys, Chinese knick-knacks and manilla shawls. The fashionable drugs were ether (Paul Masson died by pressing cotton-wool soaked in ether to his nostrils, losing consciousness, and drowning in a few inches of water) and opium. Sylvain Bonmariage, using the latter in moderation, said it revealed to him the hidden sense of things.

As to the fashion in clothes, women were so corseted that the actress Germaine Gallois never accepted a sitting part but remained laced into her whalebone edifice from 8.30 in the evening till midnight. And hats were of such height and dominance that motor-cars were designed to the milliners' specifications.

In the rue Jacob, unimpressed by any fashion, Willy's country wife was only just beginning to suspect his talent; and as her suspicions grew so did her fear of talking to him about them, as children are afraid of offending the grown-up who stops his car and offers them a lift. Instead of asking, she became ashamed for him, and ashamed of herself for keeping silent. And there were more complicated threads pulling her in different directions. There was loyalty. There was the condoning – through silence – of corruption, and there was the *laissez-faire* of a young girl who found herself in a world that was none of her business.

Illness decided for her. Disillusioned, nauseated, and most definitely frightened of her husband, and, ironic contradiction, just as definitely in love with him, she gradually declined over a period of ten weeks, until Dr Julien, from the Saint-Lazare hospital, wrote to her mother to say that he did not think that he could save her life. During those weeks of illness, confined to her room, neglected by Willy, she was nevertheless visited daily by two of his friends: Marcel Schwob, beneath whose war-mask of pale eyes and caustic tongue she recognised true friendship, and Paul Masson, grey-faced hoaxer, and one-time Colonial magistrate.

Caricature by Sacha Guitry of Marcel Schwob, 'who knew everything and guessed the rest'. (*Aventures quotidiennes*)

Marcel Schwob, already an ill man at thirty, would climb the three flights two or three times a day to visit her, to keep her lying still and distract her from the pain of the cupping-glasses that bit into her stomach, by reading to her extracts from his yet unpublished stories or translations. He was a brilliant intellectual, one of the original Symbolists, an imaginative writer, a critic and an Anglophile. He was at this time translating Defoe's *Moll Flanders*. His relationship with the young girl cooped up in his friend's flat was one of *badinage*, reflected in the teasing and childish letters she wrote to him during her convalescence.

Her other visitor was Paul Masson, who, she said, 'leered like an evil-minded curate'. He was at this period responsible for drawing up a catalogue of the books in the Bibliothèque Nationale. His learning and his love of elaborate mystification led him to add to the catalogue the titles of certain erudite Latin and early Italian works which had never been written. He had already fabricated a *Notebook of My Youth* by Bismarck, which had upset diplomatic relations between France and Germany.

In spite of these two faithful visitors and her cat, Colette believes she would not have found the will to live without the arrival of her mother, to whom however she was determined never to divulge 'the conditions of my life from which I was so grievously pining away'.

With Paul Masson, 'my first grown-up
friend', painting by Forain.

Sido came and looked after her, washed her, brushed her hair, sat by her bedside, and at night slept in the adjoining dining-room. She spoke little to her son-in-law whom she always called 'Monsieur Willy'.

Colette's body craved water and seemed to droop like a flower for lack of it, so the doctor arranged for a tub to be brought to her bedside and filled by hospital porters. She was lain in it, shivering with fever and cold, and then gently put back to bed completely exhausted. Her recovery, as Dr Julien told her, was really a matter of her own choice: he could not save her unless she found the will to live. She hesitated on the brink, not sure whether it was worth the effort, but once Sido was by her side she decided to try.

When Colette was strong enough to convalesce, it was Paul Masson who accompanied her and Willy to Belle-Ile-en-Mer. He spent the daytime with her by the sea, while Willy stayed indoors sending off letters and telegrams of instructions to the legions who made up his name, and making out copious accounts in his miniscule handwriting of what he had paid out and what was owing to him. Colette believed he was obsessed by figures, and that they played an inordinate and disquieting part in his daily life.

It was the first time that she had been to the sea, and she was completely fascinated by the crustaceous life on the beach, though she never felt so at home in her admiration as she did with the river creatures and plants she knew so well. She stayed in Belle-Ile-en-Mer for three months to recover her strength, then went to her parents in Châtillon-sur-Loing, where Willy later joined her. 'Maman whirls about, adjusts her glasses, spills water and argues with Willy all day long. It makes me laugh with delight,' she wrote to Schwob. At the end of September she returned to the rue Jacob, to the Salamander stove, the Bohemian life, the social whirl, to loneliness, and to poverty.

Willy must have coined quite a lot of money from the various books – and they sold well – published under his name, and he earned 15,000 F a year from *L'Echo de Paris* for his music column; and yet, although he paid his ghost writers a pitiful sum and the flat in the rue Jacob cost him only 1400 F a year, he was not only often in debt at this period, with the bailiffs actually in his flat, but his wife was without an outdoor coat during the bitterly cold winter of 1894–5. On the one hand he enjoyed deceiving the bailiffs, by giving them any old clothes he had, and keeping his best possessions elsewhere and under another name, but on the other hand he was, as Colette says, haunted by money. It is not at all clear where or how his money was spent, and there is no evidence to show that he hoarded it.

Once over that first illness, Colette found resources of spiritual as well as physical energy to cope not only with poverty and fear, but with whatever else might confront her. Her next shock was one which her acquaintances might have foreseen.

She received an anonymous letter. Fearfully, her schoolgirl plait slung round her neck like a snake, she followed the letter's directions to a tiny flat in the rue Bochard-Saron, where she found her husband, as the letter had said she would, with Mlle Charlotte Kinceler. The girl, young as Colette herself, was taken up by many of the writers, painters and actors of the period, and was much to Willy's taste. Her language larded with naive obscenities, disdainful of her conquests, she created a *cachet* round her person which was later evoked by the single word 'Montmartre'. She was a dwarf and a hunchback. From this first meeting Colette dates 'the end of my character as a young girl, intransigent, beautiful, absurd; through her I learnt the idea of tolerance and of pretence, the consenting of pacts with an enemy'. From her dated also Colette's jealous doubts about the man she was linked to, the realisation of his many other liaisons, and her resultant misery. Though she suffered a shock at this first discovery, she writes with compassion and a certain respect for the odd little 'Lotte' Kinceler, who at twenty-six years old put a revolver in her mouth and shot herself.

But from Willy's other affairs Colette suffered passionately. This passage in *La Vagabonde*, written nearly ten years later, re-creates her jealousy:

> To go away and die, but no longer to pretend ignorance, no longer to endure the nightly waiting, the vigil when one's feet grow cold in the too-big bed, no longer to think out those plans for revenge which, born in the dark and inflated by the beatings of a lacerated heart, poisoned by jealousy, collapse at the sound of the key in the lock and feebly let themselves be mollified when a familiar voice calls, 'What? Not asleep yet?'

Soon Willy gave up any pretence, and entertained his mistresses at home.

> One day it occurred to Monsieur Willy to bring home a lively young model. When I saw her in my flat, her chestnut hair tumbling to her shoulders, when I saw her walking about my bedroom, touching everything in it with her lovely, tip-tilted fingers, putting out her tongue in my mirror, when I saw her open her frock, in a casual, accustomed manner, on her naked eager breasts and heard her explain to Monsieur Willy, to me, to the birds at the open window, what she liked best in the way of voluptuous practices, then the blood of my mother's daughter rebelled. I made the same tight-lipped face I used to make as a child at the first sign of callers, when I would run and hide in the top branches of the tallest tree; precisely the same pinched, prudish face.

But she was prepared to put up with it. Because of love? Because she had no means of existing financially without him? Because of an inability to decide? One decision she had made with determination: she would never let her mother know that she was not happy. She went to great lengths of self-denial to achieve this end; a little out of pride, but for the most part out of a deep desire not to allow Sido to suffer because of her. Instead, therefore, of taking a decisive step, she waited. She waited for hours on the landing with Kiki the cat, Kiki who 'knew the difference between tap-water and Vittel, and who ate peas one by one'. She waited for Willy to come in. She waited for Willy to go out. She waited for a miracle to deliver her. The first of the two miracles she had formulated was that she should some-how be transported back home to the woods and forests and to Sido, without doing anything about it herself. The second that Willy should stop being Willy, and love her. Neither of the two miracles came to pass, and yet through, or in spite of, her unhappiness and her loneliness, she was gradually regaining some of the hardiness of her girlhood. Paris and winter still sapped her vitality distressingly, but in the summer months, away from the city, she revived like a flowering annual.

In July of 1895 she and Willy spent a few days in her beloved Saint-Sauveur, staying at the school at the invitation of the headmistress, Mlle Olympe Terrain, who later bitterly regretted having invited them, since the lesbian headmistress in the (at that time unwritten) *Claudine à l'école* was generally assumed to have been based on her. Thirty-five years later the outraged teacher, still smarting under the 'licentious' literature of her ex-pupil, wrote to a friend: 'Yes, the more I think of it, the more I am convinced that the soul of a cat inhabits my one-time scourge.'

From Saint-Sauveur the couple went to stay with Willy's parents who were holidaying in the Jura. The family were high-minded, extremely conventional, and god-fearing, and Colette, always terri-fied of visits, was ill-at-ease and unsociable. Nor was Willy at ease in the family atmosphere in which he did not shine. His need to show off and to be admired must have sprung from his feeling of inferiority, both moral and intellectual in front of his imposing father.

Albert Gauthier-Villars had brought up his family according to the strictest moral codes, but he was also the intellectual head of that firm which later notably published Bertrand Russell, Marie Curie and Einstein. It is scarcely surprising that both Colette and Willy were overawed. However, Willy's young nephews and nieces, who were staying in the house, quickly put Colette at her ease. They dis-covered her talents where country walks were concerned, her knowledge of flowers and insects, and of how to make musical instruments with blades of grass. Not that the grown-ups were unfriendly in any way; they merely found her lack of offers to help in household matters odd, and the amount of butter and jam she spread on her bread amazing.

When not actually staying in the Gauthier-Villars' holiday house, Colette enjoyed being in the Jura. From a cheap inn she wrote with delight to Schwob that she made Willy get up at four o'clock in the morning to go cycling with her. The couple also cycled in Paris at this period, to save money. Willy had a bicycle in perfectly good condition, but Colette's was one he had won in a raffle which had neither mudguards nor brakes.

Back in Paris from the Jura that winter of 1895, and not many weeks after their visit to her school, Willy suggested that she should write down what she remembered of her schooldays. 'Don't be afraid of the spicy bits, I might make something of it; money's short.'

With Willy's sister and mother in the Jura.

The dark apartment and the smell from the stove had imposed its usual lethargy on her, she had resorted once more to idling on the divan, caressing her cat and reading. She had no inclination at all to write, but she obediently went out and bought some school exercise books, and as if she had been set some homework, sat down with indifference and began her task. And as she wrote there grew an aching nostalgia for the woods and forests she had left. She called Saint-Sauveur 'Montigny', but it was unmistakably Saint-Sauveur, and the snakes and lizards, the flowers and fruits of the forest and the riverside, were just as unmistakably those she missed so much. Carefully she omitted to give her autobiographical heroine a mother. Although she mitigated the misery she experienced living without Sido by writing to her every day, she had no intention of writing about her for Willy. But she made the heroine the schoolgirl she herself had been, farouche, quick-witted, mocking, impatient, comical, absorbed in the moment and yet aware of what was going on in the feelings and minds of others. She wrote neatly, respecting the margins, and when she had filled six exercise books she dutifully handed in her work.

Her master paid very little attention. He flicked open a few pages, said 'I was mistaken, these can't be of the slightest use', and went back to reading the more sellable manuscripts of his commissioned hacks.

Far from feeling disappointed, Colette was relieved that she had no more homework to do. She retired to her divan, to Kiki-la-Doucette, and to silence.

It was not until two years later, on their return from a visit to the Gauthier-Villars in Lons-le-Saulnier, that Willy decided to turn out the contents of his hideous, black-painted desk, and was surprised to come across the forgotten exercise books. 'Fancy,' he said, 'I thought I'd put them in the waste-paper basket.' He glanced through the first one preparatory to chucking it away, but instead opened a second and a third, called himself '*un con*' and went off to his publisher.

The publisher, Varnier, refused it. Willy decided that the story was not spicy enough. He suggested to Colette that she hot up the childishness ... a love affair between Claudine and one of the mistresses, and to poor Mlle Terrain's later dismay, between that young mistress and the Head.

Willy next took the book to Delagrave, where again it was refused; then to Simonis-Empis, with the same result. It was not until four years later that Valdagne, a reader for the publishers Ollendorf, recommended it for publication. *Claudine à l'école*, by Willy, appeared in the bookshops in 1900. Colette had joined the ghosts.

When she saw the proofs of the cover, and the preface, she laughed at the ridiculousness of it, but beneath her laughter was a deep shame, a feeling of degradation that she was allowing herself to connive at the lie, and an awful sense of camaraderie with the young men whom she had seen treated in precisely the same way: Pierre Véber, Marcel Boulestin, Curnonsky, Jean de Tinan, Jean de La Hire, Paul Barlet, Vuillermoz, Passurf, Raymond Bouyer. The cover of *Claudine à l'école* was the drawing by Emilio della Sudda of a little red riding-hood writing in a book on her knee. The wording on the cover was WILLY and below his name *Claudine à l'école*. The 'joke' preface was written by Willy and pretended that a school-girl called Claudine had written the book herself. This preface was written as a 'cod' in the usual Willy style and was taken as such. 'Of course the preface is a joke, and you weren't taken in,' Willy wrote to Rachilde.

The book was not an immediate success, but once the notices of Rachilde in *Le Mercure*, of Gaston Deschamps in *Le Temps* and Pierre Brisson in *Les Annales* came out, the publishers sold 40,000 copies in two months. The timing was judicious. The memoirs and novels that sold well at the turn of the century were those that dealt with perverted love and drug-taking in exotic surroundings or rari-fied atmospheres. *Claudine à l'école* not only had as heroine a forth-right country schoolgirl with a refreshingly down-to-earth way of expressing herself, but thanks to Willy's suggestions, two *liaisons amoureuses* with an entirely new background. The mixture proved an enormous attraction.

Colette had promised to keep silent about the deception just as she had seen Willy's other writers keep silent. Only Ernest Lajeu-nesse, of all the young talents Willy employed, ever made a fuss, wanted to be paid, and finally refused to have his work signed Willy.

It is one thing to be gullible; but these young men knew as clearly as Colette what Willy was doing. Sylvain Bonmariage, whilst admir-ing Willy, writes that when he sent his work to him for his opinion, Willy would sometimes tell him that it was no good, whilst at the same time lifting out chunks of it to insert in his own works; and that 'if he liked it enough he would put his own name to it'. Perhaps Bonmariage wanted Willy's good opinion; but there must have been many different reasons why the other young men acquiesced. Some must have above all wanted to see their work published, and being called 'Willy' was probably the only way. This means that their work was more important to them than their name, an admirable young trait that Willy exploited. Also he was paying them, though a pittance. And again, a number of them just offered him a chapter or

'While Jacques-Emile Blanche was painting the big portrait which is now in Barcelona, I tried not to fall asleep.' (*Paris de ma fenêtre*)

two and no doubt believed when the book was published that, apart from their own contribution, the rest was indeed by Willy. Did they communicate with each other? Possibly not until years later. Only Colette and Willy's ghost-secretaries, who were actually in the room where he worked, were witness to exactly what he was doing. And the secretaries were unlikely to tell. Young men employed in a small way in a big business or a government office will accept most things in the belief (sometimes not too far-fetched) that that is what business or politics is about. In any case the young and talented have no time to expose a fraud, and no knowledge of how to. They are too concerned with their work to worry too much about being cheated.

Colette's own acquiescence sprang very definitely from fear. She writes of this state of panic in many of the pages of *Mes apprentissages*, admitting that she was so terrified that she had allowed herself to play the dupe, and at the same time was filled with shame that she should have accepted the fraudulence. She was a mixture of youth in both its extremes. Sensitive, fearful, yet possessing a strong sense of morality and justice.

The portraits of the time show her with eyes lowered, and on her features – as she herself writes – 'an expression at the same time submissive, closed in, part-gentle, part-condemned'.

But fear and acquiescence did not counteract the jealousy in her nature. Jacques-Emile Blanche remembers that though she sat submissively for his portrait of her, at the sound of a carriage outside she would jump down from the dais and run to the window, where very often she would catch sight of Willy waving goodbye to a lady friend. When this happened she was so distressed that she would have fits of hysterical tears, and have to lie down and have her forehead bathed in eau-de-cologne. She was no less unsophisticated when she sat for Forain.

Intimidated by Forain, young, bearded, always laughing, I nevertheless dared ask 'Why have you given me only one eye?' – 'Doubtless because you only had one eye that day' he replied. . . .' When I sat for him, I felt isolated. His quick brilliant glance ran over me with disdain. A very young woman cannot resign herself to being looked upon as a still life.

But her real nature was throbbing underneath this appearance of a tamed creature, and the behaviour of an obedient one, in much the same way as she recognised, many years later, the newly caged panther at the zoo:

Black fire, a red crater, two golden headlights, luminous claws, a small cat's head with ears laid back, invisible in anger . . . in the time that a wave takes to smash against a breakwater, the black panther had attacked the bars of her cage, her anxious keeper, the free air, all moving forms, trees, beings, birds, of a universe from which she had been cut off only a month

ago. ... Silence. She has returned to the obscure cavern, to the torments of hell, and her cry which makes the house tremble has not troubled the pair of lions, her neighbours. In how many months, years, of captivity had they acquired this kind of bourgeois serenity?

There were a few people, who knew Willy well, who recognised who was the real author of *Claudine à l'école*. Jules Renard wrote in *Le Journal* 'Willy HAVE a lot of talent' and Catulle-Mendès, poet and critic, colleague of Willy's on *L'Echo de Paris*, 'voluble, white and dripping like wax', said one night to her as she sat in the outer office of the newspaper: 'You're the author of *Claudine*, aren't you? No, no, I'm not asking you questions, don't overdo your embarrassment. ... In ... I don't know ... in twenty years, thirty years' time it will be known.' He was an awe-inspiring figure and she must have been surprised at his attention. 'Catulle Mendès', wrote Cocteau in a chapter devoted to him in *Portraits-souvenir*, 'was fat and walked lightly. His hips and shoulders undulated. A sort of airship roll propelled him along. ... He was like a lion and a turbot. ... At four o'clock Mendès ... injected drugs into his eyes, and into his thighs through his clothes. ...'

Nor was Rachilde entirely deceived about the authorship of the book she admired so much. She had written to Willy, who was a close friend, asking him if Colette had not had a hand in the writing of it. Willy's reply, after the mention of the obviously spoof preface, was, 'but what is not a spoof is that we made *Claudine*, Colette and I, together'. He tells her that after their visit to her school in 1895 he decided to write about it. 'So I made use of her notes but mostly of her conversation ... you would have been wildly amused to see her notes, which I had to (yes, had to, I assure you) play down and feminise for the sake of credibility. Before that sweetening, how tough and amusing they were in their boyish spontaneity.'

The perceptive Rachilde wrote in her notice: 'By Willy, the book is a masterpiece. By "Claudine", the same book is the most extraordinary work ever to be hatched from the pen of a beginner. ...' Colette wrote to thank her warmly for the notice, and dutifully confirmed Willy's collaboration. 'You know, for years I had a mass of notes in my diary, but I would never have dared to think them readable. But thanks to "La Belle-Doucette" (meaning Willy) who pruned and thinned the Claudinish crudities, Claudine became acceptable.'

The manuscript is not extant to prove how much of her text he had altered, because Willy later ordered his secretary, Paul Barlet, to destroy all the *Claudine* exercise books. Barlet, appalled, managed surreptitiously to save two of them, and secretly gave them back to Colette. These were *Claudine en ménage* and *Claudine s'en va*, both of which have very few of Willy's marginal comments; a suggestion here, a question there, in his tiny, secretive hand.

The success of the first book was in any case overwhelming, and Willy immediately sat his ghost-wife down to write a second without delay. '... the sound of the key turning in the lock and four hours imprisonment till I was free again ... but peace be on the hand that did not hesitate to turn the key. It taught me my most essential art, which is not that of writing, but the domestic art of knowing how to wait. To conceal. To save up crumbs. To change the worst into the not so bad. How to lose and recover in the same instant that frivolous thing, a taste for life.'

Claudine

laudine à Paris was published by Ollendorf the following year,
and Willy became the most popular and the most publicised
man in France. When a copy of this second book was sent to
the *Mercure de France* for reviewing, Colette enclosed a letter to
Rachilde: 'For heaven's sake don't mention me; family reasons,
traditions, relationships ... only Willy ... the glory to Willy! Poor
Willy-la-Doucette, if I could only pay my cobbler with the amount
per cent that I shall receive....'

Rachilde did not in fact like the second book as much and Colette
herself judged this and the fourth in the series, *Claudine s'en va* to be
the worst, but the heroine herself was by now unstoppable. There
were, according to Jean de La Hire in *Ménages d'artistes* Claudine
ice-creams, perfumes, Claudine collars (comparable to the Peter
Pan collars and cuffs of 1904) lotions, cigarettes, photographic plates
... and whilst Willy turned the key in the lock on the creator of
Claudine for four hours at a time so that she should get on with the
remunerative production of yet another book, he had thousands of
photographs of himself printed for publicity purposes, and sat for
paintings and caricatures as 'Claudine's Papa'. He now had enough
money for the couple to move to ampler accommodation in the rue
de Courcelles, where Colette was allotted two rooms to herself; a
good reading-lamp and a work-table in one; rings and bars for gym
practice in the other.

By the January of 1902 *Claudine à Paris* was playing in Paris at the
Théâtre Bouffes-Parisiens with *Claudine à l'école* as a prologue,
both adapted for the stage by Willy, Lugné-Poë and Charles Vayre;
and with Polaire as Claudine. Polaire had a fantastic success in
the part. She had been a music-hall singer of risqué songs under the
name of Emilie Zouzé until Willy renamed her. She was a young
Algerian, born Emilie-Marie Bouchaud, tinily thin, and with a
famous eighteen-inch waist. Wild, passionate, as odd as Colette on
the Parisian scene, she remained unsophisticated and from her own
standards incorruptible. Like Colette she had a distaste for the arti-

PREVIOUS PAGE Poster advertising
Claudine à Paris.

56

For Willy, whom I hate with all my sick
heart, Polaire.

57

ficial, the forced, the dishonest. 'Her flat-topped serpent-like head', wrote Cocteau, 'was counter-balanced by eyes like Portuguese oysters, glistening with pearls, salt and cool darkness. . . . She was as intense as a Yiddish insult and stood at the edge of the rink poised like a fit of hysterics.' She took her acting with the utmost serious-ness, and was more involved in being Claudine than in any love-affair.

For a sample of Willy's own way with stage dialogue it is interest-ing to quote the entrance of Maugis in the second act. Maugis was a character invented entirely by Willy as a skit on himself. He appears as a music critic in all the *Claudine* books with the exception of the first. Colette disclaims him forcibly in *Mes apprentissages*. She writes:

Maugis the woman-fancier, all lit-up with fatherly vice, lover of women and foreign drinks, scholarly, learned in music, letters, Greek, fond of duelling, sentimental, unscrupulous, who mocks as he secretly wipes away a tear, who plumps out his bullfinch belly, calls little women in underclothes 'baby', prefers the half-dressed to the naked and socks to silk stockings – that Maugis is no creation of mine.

In the play, gratuitously holding up the action, Maugis, dressed to resemble Willy, appears briefly in the beer-cellar scene in Act III. Willy's dialogue, unaided by any ghost, was as follows:

Kellner! May there by your courtesy, be set before me sauerkraut and sausages, begetters of pyrosis, and a draught of that sickly but salicylated dishwater that is, in your impudence, yclept Munich beer. O Beer of Munich! Liquid velvet! Forgive them, they know not what they drink.

During the very successful run of the play Willy had one of his least tasteful publicity ideas. He suggested that Colette should cut off her long hair (she was quite agreeable; only Sido was very upset: 'Your hair did not belong to you, I looked after it for twenty years', she wrote). Colette and Polaire, when dressed alike, could now pass as Claudine twins and Willy was able to parade them in restaurants and cafés as his brain-children. Colette didn't like it, but she was by now accustomed to indignities. Polaire found it cruelly distasteful, and shied away when people stared; though as an actress used for a publicity stunt, she was constrained to do what her employer told her. Natalie Clifford-Barney in her *Souvenirs indiscrets* writes: 'This Master of Publicity forced Colette but also Polaire to cut their hair and to appear as *Claudine à l'école* twins, in order to show off the schoolgirl passions that neither Colette nor Polaire had for each other.' Renée Hamon in her diary of the 1930s, cites Colette who was by then over fifty, as saying of Polaire, 'If I had asked her to make love she would have refused, because Polaire abhorred uni-sexuality.' But it was accepted in 1902 in the society in which they

moved that not only were Colette and Polaire having an affair with the acceptance and connivance of their Papa, but that the threesome were the trinity that made up the legend of Claudine: Willy the creator, Colette the model and Polaire the incarnation.

Quite aside from publicity and popular success, the critics hailed the *Claudine* books as fine literature. Not only Rachilde, who was a friend, and wrote in the *Mercure de France*, '*Claudine*, living, original and marvellously spirited, places Willy in the first rank of French novelists,' but many other critics recognised that a new and original character had been born; and one and all were amazed at the versatility of this genius Willy who was not only a brilliant research historian (*Le Mariage de Louis XV*) and a knowledgeable scientist (*L'Eclairage des portraits* and *La Couleur en photographie*)

but could create the vibrant character of a Claudine. 'Monsieur Willy has created a new type of heroine ... the style of the *Claudines* has an absolute purity....' 'Claudine, enigmatic, disturbing, incorporating eternal woman in her small person....' '... that immortal Claudine whom his heart has created more than his mind or his artistic talent, that Claudine with whom the whole world is in love, whose joyous and melancholy immorality is neither perverse nor licentious, but springs from the mad and indomitable high spirits of the graceful and intelligent animal that she is.' 'She is adorably scandalous, intelligent and vicious. Her precocity and the rarity of her perversion appal, her charm and her wit ravish.' 'I would not give this book to a woman, wife or daughter for whom I had any respect, however great the magic of its style, more, *because* of it.'

Whilst Willy collected and filed his notices and the huge pile of fan-letters, mostly from schoolgirls all of whom felt they were Claudine, the authoress coped with her loneliness as best she could. She gives a strange backward glimpse of herself at this time, in her *Journal à rebours* written in 1941: '... the day when necessity put a pen into my hand, and in exchange for the pages I wrote gave me a little money, I understood that every day, slowly, docilely, I would have to write, patiently reconciling sound and beat, get up early for preference and go to bed late from duty. A young reader need know nothing more of the good little recluse of a writer hiding behind her voluptuous novel.'

She was accompanied in her loneliness now, not only by her cat, but by the emotional little French bulldog Toby-Chien, who was to figure in a number of her books, and is the leading character in *Dialogues de bêtes*.

... her favourite companions a dog and a cat [wrote Natalie Clifford Barney], chosen no doubt because of their remarkable resemblance to their mistress. Wasn't her nature composed of these two animal natures? Obedient and devoted to a master, but secretly using the instinct of the untamed creature who escapes from all domination. She took them to the Bois for long walks, wearing high button boots, and in their flat I was intrigued by a small gymnasium, where she practised regularly at the bar, trapeze and rings – perhaps with a view to a future music-hall.

During those lonely and neglected hours in the rue de Courcelles, one of Willy's ghosts who also worked as one of his secretaries, out of kindness brought to her room a number of his young men friends to amuse her. They were all homosexuals, all beautifully dressed, and most of them English. Colette had missed the company of young men so much that, silent though she remained, 'faithful to their concept of me as a nice piece of furniture', she enjoyed their

'I exercised my body in the way that prisoners, though they have no thought of escape, cut and plait a sheet.' (*Mes apprentissages*)

laughter and their strange talk, and felt accepted by them. As late as 1932, in *Le pur et l'impur* she could still recall with immediacy what they had meant to her at that time.

I do not confide in you except to tell you about my fear of being alone. You are the most human people I know, the most reassuring in the world. If I call you freaks then what word can I use to describe the so-called normal conditions that were foisted upon me? Look there, on the wall, the shadow of that frightful shoulder, the expression of that vast back and that neck swollen with blood. ... O freaks, do not leave me alone. ...

The freaks took little notice of her, they simply used her workroom as a meeting place or played around together in the gymnasium.

Although she found their talk and their stories odd, she accepted without question what she learned of their loves and their jealousies. These were passions she could understand, and she drew no line of moral judgement between their feelings and her own. Throughout her life she took no notice of conventions, which always remained outside the moral code formed by her own nature. It was the shattering by Willy, not of any convention, but of her own sense of morality that had shocked her so deeply, in the dishonesty of his daily and

'Working for him, near him, taught me to distrust him, not to know him better.' (*Mes apprentissages*)

professional dealings, as well as in the deviousness of his promiscuity. Colette's later reputation for being shocking herself, in her books, her stage appearances and her loves is ironic, and springs from this incompatibility between her intuitive sense of morality and the conventions formed by society.

Her own anxious morality was certainly in evidence during these early years of Claudine's success: whilst the play was running she had completed the third book of the series, *Claudine amoureuse*, and it had been accepted for publication in the February of 1902.

Before the book was sent to the publishers, she wrote to Jeanne Muhlfeld begging her and her husband Lucien to stop Willy from re-writing the character of Rézi to resemble libellously his latest mistress. After dining at the Muhlfelds Willy had sat up all night, and when he went out the next morning Colette had looked at her manuscript and found what he had been doing.

... this vengeful fellow, having had a serious quarrel (I told you he had!) with G R-D, is in the process of transforming with brutal strokes the Rézi of *Claudine* into Georgie. She's in it – she would be in it! Appallingly recognisable. He mustn't do it. It's unworthy of him and of everyone else. I'm worried, as you see, and especially for him. I have my own reasons for caring less about ... Claudine's friend. My dear friend, you know that one word from you or from both of you, would stop Willy committing this. Say I've told you about it. You will be doing him a real service, and do it soon.

The Muhlfelds did nothing at all – or else they failed to influence Willy; the manuscript went to the publishers, and when, two months later, the first edition came from the presses, Mendel, the managing director of Ollendorf, ordered its destruction. He had suddenly taken fright at the possible consequences of the indiscretions in the book which involved not only Willy's Georgie, but other well-known people of the day.

Within a month, however, with as many as 562 cuts and corrections to the text, the book was published by the *Mercure de France*, re-titled *Claudine en ménage*. And in the same year Colette, still locked in her room for her four-hour stint, was writing the fourth of the series, *Claudine s'en va*.

This book has Bayreuth as part of its background, and in September she and Willy were there attending the Wagner festival, as they had every year since their marriage, at the expense of his newspaper. Willy, though he may not, as Debussy asserted, have known what a semibreve was, was very moved by Wagner's operas. Colette teased him when she discovered he was crying, but she also wrote in *Mes apprentissages* that even in daily life he had a terrifying gift for tears. Willy probably enjoyed crying at the opera, but he spent the mornings in a fever of impatience, waiting in their lodgings for his many informants to bring him the necessary material which would make up his column. She herself did not like Bayreuth, though she admired the magnificent singing voices. She loathed the place itself, the shops dedicated to Wagneriana: picture postcards, holy grails and statuettes; the thick smoke blurting from the factory chimneys, and the gasometer-like opera-house, if the opinions so tellingly held by Annie in *Claudine s'en va* can be taken to be her own. As with the other *Claudine* books this one mixes real with imaginary people and real backgrounds with imaginary situations and dialogue.

There is hardly any narrative in any of these books; their development is in the relationships and the day-to-day feelings of the characters – neither of which remain static. But Colette was still writing to order, she had not as yet chosen a subject herself, she was still under guidance from her tutor, and still having to vulgarise and titillate. And whilst Willy was keeping her hard at work, he was in his own way working no less hard himself. Before the publication of the book early in 1903, he was keeping his publicity fanned with revue sketches and mimes. He saw to it that every new revue that came out in Paris had a sketch or a skit on Willy and Claudine. 'Claudine et l'apache', 'Claudine s'amuse', 'Claudine aux arrêts', 'Claudine en vadrouille'.

The fourth book was as popular as the others and with what must have been a considerable monetary success Willy bought for Colette, and in her name, a beautiful property near Besançon in the Franche-Comté: Les Monts-Boucons. Here she lived from June till November for three consecutive years, alone but for a visit from Willy from time to time to oversee the property, his wife, and her work.

The arrangement suited them both. Colette had many of the things she craved and had been deprived of for some years. Apart from her body's necessity to breathe fresh air, the property itself, with its flowers, its old overblown orchard and its wild-life, including some goshawks nesting in the garden, recuperated her stifled senses. There were her own animals, Toby-Chien and Kiki-la-Doucette, and a local unattached cat who adopted and followed her like a dog, as is the way with the Pégot cats of the Franche-Comté; and there was the surrounding countryside reminiscent of her childhood in Saint-Sauveur. She bought for herself an ill-treated and sick horse, cared for him, rode him when she had cured his weals, and later attached him to a little cart in which she rode with the rest of her animals, ambling by hedgerows, picking wild nuts and fruit. She had hours in which to write, and arranged them with punctuality and care. She began work on four short stories about animals.

As for Willy, he was unhampered by a wife in his flat for five months of the year. Curiously whenever he came to see her he brought with him trunk loads of pornographic books because, he said, they were too valuable to leave unattended, and took them back with him each time he returned to Paris.

For the winter months Colette went back to the rue de Courcelles with him, and here, early in 1904, she wrote, to please herself, 'Minne', a short story of novella length, and for the first time asked

Les Monts-Boucons – 'all this is yours'. (*Mes apprentissages*)

to have it published under her own name. Willy very naturally for commercial reasons wanted it made into a full-length novel, and under *his* name. The *Claudine* series was finished; it was time to start on another. They fought over both issues, and she lost. In fact the two issues were of an entirely different nature, the lesser one being Colette's wish to use her own name. At twenty-nine, she was pitting her need to stand independently of him against his determination not to relinquish his success, his popularity and his dominance. Though she was sickened with submission he had more practice at winning and at destroying an opponent, and a much greater need than she to win.

But by far the greater issue for her was one which Willy would never have been able to comprehend. It is doubtful whether she had formulated it clearly enough at the time to voice it to him, and if she had, whether she *would* have voiced something which would lay her wide open to his contemptuous mockery. This issue was the fight for Minne herself, the fight to retain the spontaneous essence of the creature she had imagined. Willy was determined that this slight creation should be puffed out into a full-blown portrait with all the necessary titillations and extensions that he believed his readers had come to expect of him. Selling has little importance to a young artist, whose deepest need is to create: 'I want to say, say, say, everything I know, everything I think, everything I sense, everything which delights and hurts and astonishes me,' she wrote only a year later in *Les Vrilles de la vigne*. She had a desperate need to give birth to Minne as she saw her, by the light of her own truth and imagination. To distort a character she had honestly conceived was extremely painful, the more so since she herself was the person expected to do the distorting. She was experiencing consciously for the first time what it was to be an artist. Instinctively she knew that the character she had hoped to bring to light would be lost for ever. One can no more re-create an inspiration than one can re-create a child. She did, in fact, try very hard, in *L'Ingénue libertine* to give her heroine what she had dreamed of for her. But it was not a success. And although this later version was signed by her name alone, she was never satisfied with it.

For all the outward dressing, presentation, sharpening of outline that a Willy can give to an immature talent, it can only be excessively painful to the recipient of the favour, and though the distorted foetus may appeal to the public taste, it will nevertheless remain an unnatural freak to its author. Colette wrote in *Mes apprentissages* that Minne would never again find the agreeable little face that she had before her 'crisis of belief'. To *believe* in a fictional character was something that would never have entered Willy's mind. His friend Sylvain Bonmariage writes: 'Willy believed in nothing, not even in truth.'

The basic issue then was the cry of the creator versus the hunger for success. These opposing forces are sometimes found warring in one person, and as they are irreconcilable, one force will eventually take sway over the other; in the case of Colette and Willy they were the deepest differences in their natures. Colette communed with what she found inside herself, just as she communed with the manifestations of nature; she had never found it relevant to be watched. In fact her whole training as a child as well as her inherited instinct was to *look*. Willy above all needed to be *seen*. He had never known the instinct to create. He was a critic, an appreciator, a manipulator, never an artist. His need to be recognised was so great that among the myriad reproductions of himself that he had made into postcards by the thousand – drawings, caricatures, portraits, statuettes, cardboard effigies, wooden likenesses, etc – there was a marble cross, and resting on it a full-size head of himself with sculptured clusters of rays emanating from it. No wonder that Sacha Guitry wrote in *Gil Blas* in 1904: 'There is only God (and possibly Alfred Dreyfus) who are as well-known as he.'

Saint Willy – a publicity photo.

Of course Willy won; he was bound to. But Colette had begun to resist instead of 'to save up crumbs, to turn the worst into the not so bad'. *Minne* was published under his name, and as a new heroine, to be a good investment, must have a sequel, so was *Les Egarements de Minne*.

There exists a copy of *Minnie* 'by' Willy, published in 1904, on the title page of which is written in Colette's own hand (though obviously much later):

The original manuscript of *Minne* no longer exists. It was a short story, and in my humble opinion, better than the novel. It consisted of only one of Minne's escapades, after which the adolescent girl returned to her home before daybreak and went quietly to bed. But the signatory wanted, after four *Claudines*, another novel, and three hundred pages. He had them – as you see. Then the same person wanted me to lead Minne astray. And I led her astray. I am not proud of having done so – quite the contrary.

Some six years after the publication Colette wrote to Lucien Solvay when she was on tour in Brussels:

At the time when Willy did me the doubtful honour of signing my books, he sometimes inserted in the text a few lines destined to satisfy his personal spite. It is what he called collaborating. In *Minne* this collaboration consisted in giving Apaches the names of some estimable colleagues, notably yours. In recovering possession of *Minne* and *Les Egarements de Minne* under one title, *L'Ingénue libertine*, my first care has been to wipe out this impropriety. . . .

Willy and Colette in the rue de Courcelles. 'I waited for something final, knowing that I would not be the one to put an end to my misery.' (*Mes apprentissages*)

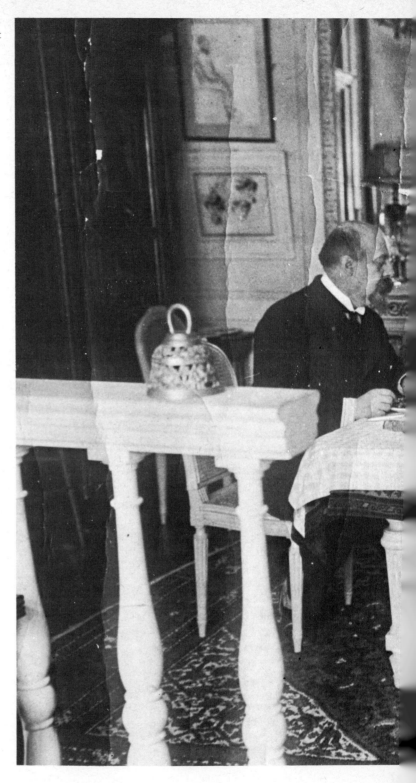

In the book Willy had called Solvay 'Solvey, known as Pipi-the-Viper, a Belgian bookmaker'.

To counteract her misery over *Minne*, Colette concentrated on her four short stories of animals. Willy, she judged, and judged rightly, would not want to put his name to anything so patently uncommercial and unsophisticated. Alone in Les Monts-Boucons she finished them, and in the same year, 1904, as *Minne* appeared, *Dialogues de bêtes* was published, under the name of Colette Willy. Willy was right: it was not a commercial investment, but it had a certain prestige success; and when the following year she added three more animal stories (the new publication was titled *Sept dialogues de bêtes*), her friend Marcel Schwob, at her tentative request, asked the poet Francis Jammes if he would write a preface.

Jammes agreed at once. A well-known and highly thought-of poet and novelist, he had by 1904 already published more than a dozen books. He lived in a very different world from the Parisian writers whom Colette knew at this time. She had a high regard for him, and the themes on which he wrote touched all the things in her that her Parisian life lacked. He wrote of animals, plants, old buildings and enclosed gardens and, more surprising to her, and just as near her heart, he wrote with tenderness and gratitude of a child's love for his mother. Strangely, with that odd mixture that runs through Colette's books of combining real people with imaginary ones – in *Claudine s'en va* Polaire was to be found at Bayreuth with the imaginary characters of Annie, Léon and Marthe – Claudine, in *Claudine à Paris*, had an unlikely passion for Francis Jammes.

Schwob himself, who had been so generous with his time and attentions to Colette during her long illness, was now, during the last two years of his life, confined to his bed in the rue Saint-Louis-en-l'Ile. She visited him often, sat on the floor by his bedside, and played with his ménagerie: a bat, a dormouse, a lizard, a squirrel, a grass-snake. Though his intellectual brilliance and her earthy intuition might seem to have nothing in common, they had an instinctive and genuine friendship. There was no-one, however, at this time, including his wife, the actress Marguerite Moreno, later her closest friend, to whom Colette would have confided the deceptions of her daily life. Having sworn to herself not to confide in Sido, there was no-one nearer, and she kept her miseries both proudly and ashamedly to herself.

Paradoxically one of her greatest fears was the fear of displeasing Willy, even if pleasing him meant forfeiting the regard not only of others, but of her own self, though at the time of *Minne*, she knew that neither collaboration nor marriage itself was any longer possible for either of them. She was slow to relinquish the latter. What she wanted was the conjugal dream, and she was obstinate enough not to give in to the fact that with Willy this was impossible. He could not change. She was the one who would have to change, and as it was impossible for her any longer to change to accommodate him, she would have to change into someone capable of living by herself, not only morally and physically, but in the basest material sense. She had no possessions, and as far as any publisher knew, she had no profession. Indeed in the bibliography at the back of Jean de La Hire's book *Ménages d'artistes*, written at this time, after a long list of books attributed to Willy including of course the four *Claudines* and the two *Minnes*, comes the following: "Colette Willy: *Dialogues de bêtes, and certain journalistic collaborations, notably 'Notes musicales'*". It would take her a long time and arduous work to establish the fact that she was a writer. In the meantime consciously or unconsciously she had been preparing physically for another profession.

Whether it was at her request or due to his own prescience, Willy had paid for her to have dance and mime lessons with Georges Wague, who was not only a teacher and choreographer, but was also one of the best-known mime dancers on the stage. He was born Georges Vaag in 1885 in Paris, and had started his pantomime career at the Café Procope when he was eighteen. He was totally professional, and remained a partner to Colette throughout her music-hall career, and a life-long friend. Apart from these first lessons which she attended at the Mimi Pinson School of Modern Pantomime – for which Willy paid 120 F for twelve lessons – she had also been appearing in a few amateur performances of plays in the homes or gardens of their friends. On the lawn of Natalie Clifford-Barney's house in Neuilly she had played a faun in a sketch which was said to have been written by Willy, but which was, in fact, written by one of his henchmen. She was not entirely successful, and it was evident to her audience that she could never become a professional actress, because although her body was supple and she had a young animal warmth, her strong Burgundian accent was not an asset. On this occasion in any case the performance was scarcely over when something more calculated to be sensational caught the audience's attention. A nude woman on a white horse slowly approached from the other end of the lawn, who surprised Colette not by her nudity – though that may have been the horsewoman's intention – but by her skin which, uncovered by stage body-make-up, was of a mottled purplish and ugly unevenness. This apparition was a Dutch woman named Margaretta Geertruida Zeller, later McLeod, who purporting to be an Indian dancer was the sensation of Paris and other European capitals at that time, under the exotic name of Mata Hari. If Colette were thinking of a stage career, she would have a great deal of this sort of sensationalism to vie with. But she was not, in fact, thinking very seriously of it.

Though both she and Willy knew it was time for her to go she lacked the courage to leave, allowing herself to dream of flight but never to attempt it. It was obvious to Willy that he must take the first step, but why he should wish to get rid of her now that she was his chief ghost, his chief source of income, can only be attributable to his own deviousness. Perhaps he was unbearably weary of her. Or did he believe, as it seems he did by his later behaviour, that he could keep his professional hold on her and count on her silence, without having any longer to put up with her in his home? However he felt about it, he set about getting rid of her with his usual games-manship, his marital games being played with no less relish than his literary ones. He wished her to find him out at the same time as professing innocence; he wished her to overhear snatches of telephone conversation at the same time as he feigned guilt as he replaced the receiver.

Colette by now had recognised the games as such quite consciously, and she had to confess to herself that what had been a passion great enough to have made her suffer considerably, however mixed it had been with fear and shame, was now only a habit which she was frightened of relinquishing. 'One only dies from the first man,' she wrote in *Mes apprentissages*. And in *Le Pur et l'impur*: 'That man always comes into our lives more than once. His second apparition is less frightening, for we had thought him unique in the art of pleasing and destroying; by reappearing he loses stature . . . he knows that he is stripped of his powers the minute a woman, in talking about him, says "they" instead of "he".'

But Willy was the first man and had the power not only to demean her but to destroy utterly her self-respect. She found herself submitting without resistance to the degrading game of taking one of his mistresses out for the day whilst he entertained another.

And yet she waited. There were no rows, nothing had in fact changed in their lives, she could tell herself. There was no reason why, after twelve years of knowing that he had affairs with other women, she should suddenly revolt.

Was it love that kept me with him? When a passion is really the first it is hard to say 'at this hour, of this blow, love died'. How old was I? Twenty-nine? Thirty? The age when you can no longer die for anyone or because of anyone. Thirty already. And already that hardening that I would compare with the crust that lime springs form, dripping slowly. One by one the warm drops trickle from your forehead to your feet, and you are scared: 'Why it is blood; my blood.' But it is not blood. It is the petrifying water slipping down, leaving as it dries a fine powdery ash that gradually thickens. So do the aged crabs put on their coats of lime and the ancient, ancient lobsters dozing beneath the rocks, grey and stony and almost invulnerable.

She was very far from invulnerable but there was a strong pride in her which did not wish to admit that she had not been happy; there was Sido to tell; there was the thought of living without protection or a livelihood in those pre-1914 days when to desert the domestic hearth, as the Napoleonic Code called it, was a cold and lonely step to take. And she was thirty. To begin a new life at thirty was a great deal to ask of life and of herself. When, however, Willy, tired of hints, said after one of her amateur performances, 'If you would like to appear in a real theatre, I am sure it would be easy for you to arrange some pleasant little trips' and suggested that Brussels and other touring engagements would be a good idea as it would enable him to get rid of the flat they shared and to lead a different kind of life, she could no longer pretend that the marriage was not at an end. Even then she did not hurry. She only tentatively looked for a place to live in whilst she stayed on in the rue de Courcelles in silence.

Missy

IN JANUARY 1906 SHE FOUND THE courage to move to a ground-floor flat in the rue de Villejust. In one way she felt so immediately free and trusting that she left her key without thinking in the outside of the lock when she went to bed that first night. In another way she was so fearful that she jumped at every sound of the doorbell. Willy had immediately begun sending her notes, but they were not notes that even so much as hinted that she should come back (and at this stage she might even gratefully have done so); the notes were all adamant demands for the return of the manuscript in her writing that she had taken with her. He had kept the rest of them, those which he later ordered Paul Barlet to destroy. Sylvain Bonmariage claims that immediately after the separation Colette set about trying to smear Willy's reputation, and that Willy himself never had any thoughts of revenge; but since the peremptory notes she received at this time included one that said 'I am so made that with me *spite* is the ardent counterpart to gratitude', it would seem that Bonmariage was a little over-zealous in the defence of his friend. Colette, released from her chains, may well have felt vengeful, but it was not until thirty years later, five years after Willy's death, that she told the story of her bondage, and that of his other ghosts, in *Mes apprentissages*. Meanwhile, true to his strange form, Willy sent her one note which instead of menacing her, asked her in just such terms as she knew he asked Curnonsky, Boulestin, Véber, and the others, for twenty descriptive pages for his new novel 'such as you know how to write', and to her enormous surprise offered her one thousand francs. The sum was a great deal more than she had received for the four *Claudine* novels put together, but with unquestioning integrity she felt obliged to turn it down because the description was to be of Monaco, which she hardly knew and anyway disliked. The always surprising Willy then telegraphed her: 'If the novel has for background the Franche-Comté will you accept? If yes, the action will emigrate to eastern regions.'

At the same time this curious man sent on to her the bills she had

PREVIOUS PAGE 'The reassuring presence of Missy.' (Letter to Hamel)

incurred during the time she was with him. Colette sent them back to him, not only because she had not enough money to pay them, but because she believed that they were his responsibility. Willy's subsequent games were in his own inimitable style. He was earning a huge sum from his many ghosted books – since the *Claudines* anything signed Willy was an assured success – and a fair amount from his theatre collaborations; but he had so arranged things with his friends that a proportion of his royalties was slipped to him 'under the counter', as he explained to Bonmariage, so that neither Colette's nor his own creditors could be paid, although he could still live in the style he wished.

For Colette, alone in the rue de Villejust, the beloved solitude and freedom she had not known for thirteen years had taken the place of loneliness and the locked room; but this time tempered with regret for the warmth of his body beside her in bed, for the crook of his arm where she slept, for the might-have-been, for companionship. She was not however without the companionship of animals. Toby-Chien and Kiki-la-Doucette at first accompanied her, though later Toby-Chien went to live with one of Willy's secretaries, because, emotional child that he was, neither Willy nor she wished to deprive him of the other's company. She then acquired her first French bulldog bitch, Poucette, and a female Belgian sheepdog, Belle-Aude.

After her life with Willy, Colette, like her mother, favoured female animals – 'La Chienne-bull' and 'La Chatte' with different names and alive at different dates, figure henceforth throughout her life.

So many favourite animals had she that she dreamed her fear of forgetting one.

'Who's barking?'

'Me.'

'Who's me? A bitch?'

'No. *The* bitch.'

'Of course, but which?'

'Is there another one then? You always called me THE bitch. I am the dead one.'

'Yes, but forgive me, which one? Are you Nell?' (Silence.)

'No, I am not Nell.'

'Oh, have I hurt you?'

'No, not much . . .'

'Oh! What am I thinking of! Of course, you're Lola!'

(A long silence.)

'Alas! I am not Lola.'

'Wait! I know! You're . . .'

She wakes before she can remember which one she has forgotten . . .

'The peace of our garden' – Sido and the Captain.

At one time she was to be seen cycling daily in the Bois de Boulogne in her Zouave bloomers and the cloth cap which the Comtesse de Noailles called her 'old hunter's hat' with Belle-Aude trotting beside her, and Pati, a minuscule toy terrier in her bicycle basket. She liked to surprise people as she lifted the tiny bitch to the ground by calling out in a coarse accent, which the animals obeyed only if she shouted in this way: 'On yer *raite*, if yer please, on yer *raite*.' More than one passer-by stood stock still with amazement that the two dogs could so promptly distinguish their right from their left.

At the time of Colette's separation from Willy, her father, Jules-Joseph Colette, died.

He was given the handsomest of village funerals, a coffin of yellow wood covered only by an old tunic riddled with gashes – the tunic he had worn as a Captain in the First Zouaves – and my mother accompanied him steadily to the grave's edge, very small and resolute beneath her widow's veil, and murmuring under her breath words of love that only he must hear. We brought her back to the house, and there she promptly lost her temper with her new mourning, the cumbersome crèpe that caught on the keys of doors . . . she was dry-eyed, flushed and feverish. . . . A kitten came in, circumspect and trustful, a common and irresistible kitten four or five months old. He was acting a dignified part for his own edification, pacing grandly, his tail erect as a candle, in imitation of lordly males. But a sudden and unexpected somersault landed him head over heels at our feet, where he took fright at his own temerity . . . then spun round like a top. And she laughed, sitting there in her mourning, laughed her shrill young girl's laugh, clapping her hands with delight. Then, suddenly, searing memory . . . dried the tears of laughter in her eyes.

Later in a letter to Colette, Sido wrote: 'Oh, what a child he was! And what a pity he loved me so much! It is his love for me which wiped out his beautiful aptitude for literature and the sciences. He preferred to think only of me, to torment himself on my account, and that's what I find unforgivable. Such a great love! What levity! As for me, how should I console myself for the loss of such a loving friend.'

Colette did not spend all her time alone with animals in the rue de Villejust. She wrote in an angry letter to Charles Saglio, the editor of *La Vie parisienne*, whom she accused of leaving the office on purpose when she was due to arrive with the manuscript of a short story, countering his excuse that he didn't know how to get hold of her: 'When I'm not to be found at 44 rue de Villejust, one goes to No. 2 rue Georges-Ville, a seven-month-old baby knows that.'

In the rue Georges-Ville, where for the next few months she spent a great many of her days, and nights, lived the Marquise de Belbeuf, known to her select circle of friends as 'Missy'. The Marquise, who was separated from her husband, was the youngest daughter of the Duc de Morny, a great-grand-daughter of the Empress Joséphine and a niece of Napoleon III. Her mother, the Princess Sophie Troubetzkoi had found her so unattractive as a child that she had left the whole of her upbringing to the servants on the estate. A highly

Colette and Missy: 'You seem so far away'. (*Les Vrilles de la vigne*)

intelligent, quiet, strong and delicate-minded girl, she had, after one botched night – so rumour had it – with her husband the Marquis, eschewed the company of men and loved only women. She dressed like a man, either in dinner jacket when she was entertaining (exclusively women) or in mechanics overalls during the day; and was adept at all kinds of technical-manual work. Her hair was cut like a man's and she was in fact deceptively male to look at. It was one of Willy's jokes to sit in a Ladies Only compartment of a train, and, when questioned, to reply: 'I am the Marquise de Belbeuf.'

Missy was the admired and respected centre of a clique of women who met at each other's houses or in bars and restaurants, who dressed as men and had mannish tastes in cigars, monocles and carnation buttonholes. Some of them had love relationships, not so much among themselves as with younger protégées; some of them lived this life romantically but without passion, some out of a dislike of men, some out of shyness of the opposite sex, and some purely for companionship. Lépine, the Paris Prefect of Police did not allow them to wear men's clothes in public so like naughty schoolgirls they would cover their attire with long cloaks when they took a cab to their rendezvous. They were all from the higher échelons of society: Baronesses, Cannonesses, grand-nieces of Tsars ... Missy seems to have been the most notable and at the same time the most remote of them; and when Colette, who was much younger than she, and indeed than the others, went to live alone, the Marquise befriended and appropriated her, watched over her, and paid for anything she might need. Jules Renard noted in the *Journal* that Colette wore a bracelet at this time on which was engraved 'I belong to Missy'.

Though Colette shared a bed with her friend, her relationship with Missy remained ambiguous. What she sought was total refuge in gentleness and sensitivity after the coarseness of the 'laborious sexual pastime' and 'the shadow of that frightful shoulder, the expression of that vast back and the neck swollen with blood' of her earlier experience. It was like a reprieve from sex whilst allowing for the passion, affection and care of a deep relationship. Her friend 'X' as she calls him in *Le Pur et l'impur* was 'the first to designate, in a word, my place in the scheme of things. I believe he assigned to me the place of a spectator; he felt I should have one of those choice seats that allow the spectator, when excited, to rush on to the stage, join the actors, and take part in what is going on. I was not fooled for long by those photographs that show me wearing a stiff mannish collar, necktie, and short jacket over a straight skirt, a lighted ciga-rette between two fingers.... How timid I was at that period when I was trying to look like a boy, and how feminine I was beneath my disguise of cropped hair.' Of the Marquise, in the same book, she writes, '... the salacious expectations of women shocked her very natural platonic tendencies, which resembled more the suppressed excitement, the diffuse emotion of an adolescent, than a woman's explicit need. "I do not know anything about completeness in love," she said, "except the *idea* I have of it."'

Colette quotes, too, the far from amorous conversations of other members of the clique, talking to their young protégées: 'Have you learnt your Chopin Waltz yet?' ... '... tut tut, my sweet, one doesn't cut a baba with a knife, use the small fork' ... 'What do you mean by putting your husband into a bad temper by going home late every night?'

To a great many of these women sex had much less importance than the other necessities of a close relationship. Dominance and subservience; protectiveness and protection; jealousy and confidence, faithfulness and faithlessness; argument, prickliness and the forgiving gentleness of the touch of a hand.

Colette wrote with authority on Proust's Gomorrha.

Since Proust has thrown light on Sodom, we feel respect for what he has written of. We would no longer dare to meddle with these hunted creatures.... But – was he misled, was he uninformed? When he assembles a Gomorrha of unfathomable and vicious young girls, denounces a frenzy of bad angels, we are only amused and care little, having lost the consolation of the overwhelming truth which guided us through Sodom. Because, with due respect to Marcel Proust's imagination, there is no Gomorrha. Puberty, college, solitude, prison, aberration, snobbism, are meagre nursery-gardens, insufficient to engender and store a manifold and well-established vice, and its necessary solidarity. Intact, enormous, eternal, Sodom contemplates from on high its puny, underdeveloped imitation.

And yet in the story 'Nuit blanche' Colette wrote that when she needed to have her 'demons of fever, of anger, of disquiet, calmed': 'your kiss will hold me more firmly, your hands become more loving ... you will give me sensual pleasure, leaning over me, your eyes full of maternal anxiety, you who search, through your passionate friend, for the child you never had'.

What seemed to Parisians outrageous behaviour on the part of a woman was to Colette as natural as the play of puppies, or the necessity of a mother's goodnight kiss, and satisfied equally as natural demands. She could not of course have ignored the fact that she was behaving outside convention, but since that convention was alien to her she saw it for what it was: the code of behaviour of a particular set of people. She had been brought up under a different code, so she was not to her own mind breaking any fundamental rules.

Her very natural sensuality and sexuality had developed as any other uninhibited country girl's. At twelve she had been as terrified of sex between human beings as of death or illness. She shut out the horror of it; and did not want to associate it with the copulations she saw among the animals in her own life.

At the back of the farmhouse one window is open and lighted up...
'That's the bedroom for the married couple!' whispers Julie. The bedroom for the married couple. . . . I had not thought of that. . . . They will sink into that mound of feathers, the heavy shutters will be closed upon them, and the door and all the exits of that stifling little tomb. Between them will be enacted that obscure encounter of which my mother's out-

'With such distinguishing marks as pleated shirt front, sometimes a waistcoat, and always a silk pocket handkerchief, I frequent a dying society.' (*Le Pur et l'impur*)

spoken simplicity and the lives of the animals around me have taught me too much and too little. And afterwards? I am frightened of the room, of the bed that I had never thought of.... 'Where are you going? Where are you off to?' I have fled, trampling on the lettuces, and the raised ridges of the asparagus bed. 'Wait for me! What on earth's the matter with you?'

Julie does not catch me up until I have reached the gate of the kitchen garden and the red halo of dust surrounding the lights of the dance floor. There, close to the re-assuring hall that resounds with the tumult of the blaring trombone, of laughter and stamping feet, her impatience finally extorts the most unexpected of answers, bleated amid floods of tears by a bewildered little girl: 'I want to go home to Maman.'

By the time she was seventeen her sexual curiosity had been aroused; but her first experience left her not only disappointed but miserable and frightened.

And yet she had remained totally faithful to Willy during the thirteen years of their marriage; and she was thirty-one by the time they parted. Her attitude to faithfulness is made understandable by a much later conversation reported in Renée Hamon's diary. Renée had confessed to being in love with a woman to whom 'she would be faithful for ever'. 'You are no more faithful than I am,' she quotes Colette as saying to her that evening. 'You are monogamous in the way that I am. You are faithful because you cannot divide your love. I know about that. ... I couldn't make love to anyone else, whilst the old love existed.'

A few months after she left Willy, her dance teacher, Georges Wague, asked her to appear with him and his wife in a mime drama, *Le Désir, l'amour et la chimère*. These danced stories, mostly of melodramatic or exotic flavour, were fashionable in Paris at the time, and though Colette's accent narrowed her chances of being cast in a play, there was no reason why she should not appear in a mime. Even before the famous scandal in January of the following year, a great many people who had known her as Willy's wife censored her for this new profession.

But Colette had a very real need to earn her living, and also to stretch out bodily and mentally, to reassert physically her *joie de vivre* after the long restrictions of artificiality and unhappiness. The repressed animal warmth and vigour which were deeply embedded in her and which had so nearly not survived in the early days of Willy's Paris, speedily surfaced. Though still suffering from a fear of her fellow-creatures she was young enough to recover quickly, and she flung herself into her role, and indeed all her subsequent ones, with total absorption. Wague, interviewed by the newspaper *Le Capitole* said of her: 'She obtained the maximum of exteriorisation

Missy and Colette – Willy's comment: 'dislocation of aristocrats'.

85

of thought, with her eyes closed.' The honesty of bodily work, and the becoming someone else, left her no time for memories or regrets. Acting, though it may seem to be a most glaring exposure, she found in fact was its very opposite: 'Very quickly there came to me that odd sensation that only on the stage was I really alone and safe from my fellow-creatures, protected from the whole world by a barrier of light.'

She made her début in February 1906, and in the same year appeared, also with Wague as her partner, in *La Romanichelle*, and in *Pan* at the Théâtre Marigny.

Her stage appearances had very different effects on different people. Sido had written to her when she heard she was to appear: 'I wouldn't have thought you were suited to it. You used to be rather set in your ways, and for the stage one needs to be supple both morally and physically. Though it's true you have become more adaptable.' And in another letter: 'I once told you that you had nothing that makes for success in the theatre; that you didn't know how to speak, to walk, to sit down, to come in or to go out.'

The professional critics disagreed with each other about Colette's ability:

... she gives at the same time an impression of daring and naïveté, there is something chaste in her face ... there is also something which is obviously sensuous ... she reveals her uplifted bosom and we do not know if we are disturbed or if we simply wonder at her. She wants to be touching and at the same time perverse, and we let ourselves bow down to her wishes, but we feel that in all this there is something inexplicable and something very pure.

She lacked even an elementary preparation for the profession ... every time she came down after a leap she landed heavily on her bare feet with a flat thud.

... characteristic of Colette Willy's playing is the absence of any set rules. On the contrary, an absolute and impulsive sincerity in her playing seems to come from emotions actually felt. She gives herself over completely to her part which she lives rather than plays.

Sylvain Bonmariage, meeting her after a performance of *Pan*, wrote:

She emitted an indefinable and troubling odour of sensuality. There was something in her of a panther stretching, an agility that could only belong to that same animal. She gave the impression of a wild creature even in her manner of eating. She exhaled that feeling of unashamedness that I have known in no-one else, disconcerting, sincere, direct, but which invited no man to lack respect for her. It was at the same time impudence, the absence of prejudice and an overwhelming aspiration towards the freedom of nature.

He once said to her 'How marvellously you observe people,' and she had replied, 'I don't observe anyone. To understand people I have to become them.'

Colette herself parodied her stage performances in *La Retraite sentimentale*, where Annie briefly describes dancing a pas-de-deux with 'Willette Collie', who disconcerted her by varying the steps every night and tickling her under the ribs during a passionate kiss. This last allusion was to the 'shocking' incident that Paris had taken with great seriousness earlier in the year, and which was subsequently known as 'the Scandal of the Moulin-Rouge'.

Though excessively shy Missy was very interested in the theatre and had written little revue sketches, as indeed had her father the Duc. At Colette's request Georges Wague had given mime lessons to the Marquise and the two women had rehearsed a mime ballet written by Missy called *Rêve d'Egypte*, in which she played the part of a man. The scene was Pharaoh's Egypt. A mummy awakes from eternal sleep, undoes its bandages and, near nude, dances its ancient loves.

At what moment or by whose suggestion Missy allowed herself to be persuaded to appear in public it is hard to judge. Perhaps Colette's serious involvement in the theatre had infected her too. However it was, the Moulin-Rouge presently announced on its billboards, the opening of a mime ballet written by the Marquise de Belbeuf and danced by Yssim (the press was not slow in reading the pseudonym backwards) and Mme Colette Willy. Posters were printed with the Morny coat-of-arms above the name Yssim, which highly displeased the Duc. As for the Marquise's husband, the Marquis de Belbeuf, he went in angry mood to the first night on 3 January 1907, supported by his friends from the Jockey Club. Willy of course was also present. The performance might have remained within bounds, but Colette was not a mime who 'behaved', whether circumspectly or not; she 'became' her parts, and when the lovers were united in a kiss she flung herself into the passion with her usual ardour. Not only were the Marquis and his friends outraged, but so was the whole audience. When the curtain came down they were in an ugly mood. Willy jumped on to the stage in front of the curtain and applauded ostentatiously, which cynicism so outraged them that they turned upon him with shouts and abuse so violent that he hurriedly left by an emergency exit. The scandal lost him his job on the *Echo de Paris*.

At the demand of the Morny family, the Prefect Lépine forbade a second performance, but compromised on condition that the Marquise was replaced by Georges Wague, and that the title should be changed 'for diplomatic reasons' from *Rêve d'Egypte* to *Songe*

'Rumour has it that Yssim is none other than la Marquise herself.' (Moulin Rouge Advertisement)

MOULIN ROUGE

? YSSIM ?
ET
COLETTE WILLY
DANS
RÊVE D'ÉGYPTE
PANTOMME DE
Mme la Marquise de MORNY
Intercalée dans la
REVUE DU MOULIN
2 ACTES TABLEAUX
10 REPRÉSENTATIONS SEULEMENT
Première Représentation le 3 Janvier 1907
LE BUREAU DE LOCATION EST OUVERT POUR CES REPRÉSENTATIONS

Claudine en Ménage

Dessin de SEM

I™ 1905

LA MARQUISE   COLETTE WILLY

Caricature by Sem.

d'Orient. The director came in front of the curtain before this second performance to announce that Georges Wague would dance the part of Franck, but in spite of the announcement the audience believed it was Yssim on stage, and from the moment the curtain rose there were whistles and cat-calls.

Claude Pichois, who has edited a number of collections of Colette's letters, states that the cat-calls were engineered by Willy. However this may be, it is certain from what he himself told his friends, that after the scandal of the night before he had decided to break with Colette definitively. Colette was interviewed in her dressing-room by Paul Lagardère of *Le Petit Parisien* after the performance: 'Was I nervous? No, it's not in my nature,' she said.

It is ironic that an earthy, straightforward girl should from the moment she arrived in Paris have been able to shock an 'unshockable' society with what Henry de Jouvenel later called her 'monstrous simplicity'. Willy and his like had been trying for years to be sensational, before this gauche country girl, first mildly by her social gaffes (Rémy de Gourmont wondered if she spoke them on purpose) and later in her writings (parents forebade their children to read the *Claudines*) and her stage appearances, outraged their sensibilities. The public blamed her for shattering their unnatural idea of morality. They were used to titillation, to innuendo, to the salacious and winked at. The injection of the animal-natural into their theatres and their literature was to them truly shocking. Colette bared one of her beautiful breasts in public. Beneath the cut-up strips of Paniska's costume in *Pan* was a nude Colette. This was essential to her interpretation of a faun; she knew and identified with animals too closely to attempt to interpret them corseted.

But she had no desire to be obscene. Now, as much later, her natural dignity shied at what she considered pornographic. Her different attitudes towards the homosexuals who met in her room in the Willy days, and Willy's own nastiness with sex, are exemplified in her refutation of the sexual behaviour of Willy's Maugis, that character he injected into the *Claudines*. What she considered admissible and inadmissible was not influenced by society's taste. Her mother even saw her sense of morality as inflexible, as indeed was her own, though it had nothing to do with church-going or conforming to a village moral code. And Colette's illness had been brought about as much by the shock of Willy's lack of ethics, as by the stifling Salamander stove. Nor did she change in her strictures. In 1932 in a letter to Lady Troubridge who had sent her D.H. Lawrence's novel, she wrote '... and what do you think of this poor childish excited person, the author of *Lady What-not's Lover*? It's terribly sixth-form and college ... what a narrow province obscenity is, suffocating and boring.'

Nevertheless such was the feeling in Paris against her at the time of the *scandale* that she and the Marquise retired for some time to the Marquise's villa in the Somme district. And, odd behaviour once more, Willy and his mistress, Meg Villars, the singer and dancer, rented the villa next door. It may seem strange too that Colette not long afterwards dedicated one of the stories in *Les Vrilles de la vigne* to Meg Villars; but Colette throughout her life remained friends with women whom she had reason to dislike. Her friendships, seemingly, were based on what she thought of the women them-

selves, not on their behaviour towards her.

During February 1907 the *séparation de biens* was announced between husband and wife. This division of the property belonging to each is a preliminary of divorce proceedings in France, each partner taking with him on separation only what belongs to him in the way of money and possessions. Colette of course had nothing. Les Monts-Boucons which Willy had bought for her in her name he had somehow managed to take back and sell at the moment of separation. And his self-confessed spite took one very vindictive turn before the actual divorce three years later. Colette wrote to Léon Hamel:

... he has sold, without my knowledge, all the *Claudine* books to the publishers for next to nothing,* so that these books which are so entirely mine (morally) are now lost for ever both for him and for me. One would think, given the conditions under which he has forfeited the four *Claudines* that he not only wished to make very little out of them himself, but that he is also making sure that never, even after his death, will I have possession of my own books.

I have been completely bowled over, dear friend, and I have written to tell him so. He has replied to my cry of despair with a cold, almost menacing, letter, and I believe that after the necessary explanation which will take place on his return from Monte Carlo (the day after tomorrow) everything will be finished between us.

Nearly thirty years later, she seems to have forgotten the exact circumstances of the sale, and believes she was an unwilling party to it. Here is what she remembers of it in *Mes apprentissages*.

From its first appearance *Claudine à l'école* sold well. Then better still. The *Claudine* series it seems is still selling, after hundreds of editions. ... I can only speak from hearsay ... the *Claudines*, at the time of my divorce already belonged to two publishers, Monsieur Willy having sold all publishing rights to them for a tiny sum. At the bottom of the contracts I had added my signature as wife of the author. This relinquishment is the most inexcusable gesture ever obtained from me by fear, and I have not forgiven myself for it.

Though the details are wrong, the sense of betrayal and nausea have remained and one can assume that when she did have a meeting with Willy on his return from Monte Carlo, however outraged she was, he managed to frighten her as he was still capable of doing.

But the letter to Hamel, written as it was at the very moment of her discovery of what Willy had done, is probably nearer the truth. Hamel destroyed all her numerous letters to him, presumably to protect her, but he nevertheless first copied each one into his diary. She wrote frequently to this very dear friend who was fifteen years her senior, sometimes simply wishing to confide one or two incidents to him, and adding 'what else to tell you ...'.

The little faun in *Le Desir, l'amour et la chimère*.

* Claude Pichois in a footnote to this letter states that the sum was indeed a pittance.

Hamel was a dilettante with a large inherited fortune; tall, good-looking, a sportsman and a traveller, he was also discreet to the point of self-annihilation: 'The Silent One' she called him in the short story 'Partie de pêche' that she dedicated to him in *Les Vrilles de la vigne*. She had first met him at Rozven, in Brittany, where Missy had a house. Her letters to him have the intimacy and freedom of entries in a diary; they are also affectionate, yet impersonal, letters written indeed to a trusted confidant.

She had only chanced to hear about Willy's dealings with the publishers while she was playing at the Comédie Royale in Paris in a two-act play she had written with parts for herself and her bulldog bitch Poucette, entitled *En camarades*. It was her first attempt at writing for the theatre.

Whilst she was playing in it, the *Comoedia Illustrée* asked her to write on her 'ideas on the theatre in general'. She replied frankly that she hadn't any, and that having written but one play in two acts did not entitle her to have any. But she already had very firm ideas about dialogue in the theatre, and these beliefs never changed. She wrote: 'The dialogue in *En camarades* has the loose, natural, rapid irrelevance of everyday language; the language of negligent people, people in a hurry, too lazy to speak correctly. . . .' She also thanked the other actors in print, including Poucette, though years later in writing the five last essays which make up *Dialogues de bêtes* (written a long time after the first seven) it is Toby-Chien who talks of his triumph on stage with her, at the Folies-Elyséennes; but whether this was because she forgot it was Poucette and at the Comédie-Royale, or whether she was fictionalising, or whether Toby-Chien (as she maintained he often did) was lying, it is difficult to judge.

La Vagabonde

A NEW DÉCOR WAS BECOMING FASHIONABLE in Paris in these early years of the new century, taking the place of the heavy multi-national tastes of the 'Maude, the Lianes and the Vovonnes': Art Nouveau. Maxim's was the first restaurant to be decorated entirely in this new style of elongated curly exquisiteness. Colette preferred it to the suffocating weightiness of the Nineties. In 1907 she wrote to Robert de Montesquiou-Férensac:

I've read your study of Aubrey Beardsley at least three times. I have an almost culpable passion for this very young man, so much does something hidden in me respond to his drawings. I have very few friends, Monsieur. This is certainly not a complaint! But I am told that I live a useless life, and I know that I am censured, particularly because I don't explain my reasons for having broken away from all that is good, or that passes for good.

She felt herself cast out; but what explanation could she give that would have been believed? And what, in any case, was the use of explaining to a society which accounted her life with Willy to have been *sage*?

From the beginning of her separation from him, Colette packed every moment of her life with work. Although she had a new and exhausting profession she had grown so accustomed, thanks to Willy, to doing her daily stint of writing, that the habit remained. *La Retraite sentimentale*, with its nostalgic memories of Les Monts-Boucons was published early in 1907 under the name Colette Willy. Rachilde read it just before publication in her professional capacity as critic and literary editor. In a letter to Colette she confessed to tears of enthusiasm, but added in a reference to the recent Moulin-Rouge scandal: 'Try, Colette, I beg you, to remember that you carry something precious in your mad cat brain, which jumps over the gutters of social prejudice, but that you can upset its beautiful balance by walking on your hands for instance.'

Yet even *La Retraite sentimentale* added to her reputation for being shocking.

It must have been on the strength of this one book that Eugène Gilbert wrote of her in *La Revue des deux mondes* – because surely he cannot be censoring her for her *Dialogues de bêtes*, and there was no thought at this time in the public mind that she was the author of the *Claudines*, nor by the time the review appeared had she written anything else: 'It is not without a melancholy regret,' he wrote, in his short but wordy reference to her, 'that we see great talents give the sanction of their authority to those audacities of the pen, which no matter what one says or thinks, always take away from a woman that halo of chaste gentleness and modest grace which have been, since that long ago hour when Christianity picked her up from her pagan abjection, the most seductive, the most irresistible and the least contestable of her attributes.'

anything else: 'It is not without a melancholy regret,' he wrote, in On tour only three months after the publication of *La Retraite sentimentale*, Colette sent to Charles Saglio of *La Vie parisienne* her volume of essays and stories, *Les Vrilles de la vigne*. She had written them in her dressing-room some months before during the intervals of *Pan* at the Théâtre Marigny, and it was one of these stories she had taken to show him on the day he had left the office to avoid her. The reason now became clear. Saglio, cautious even to the point of meanness in his later business dealings with her, had wanted to ask Willy for his permission before accepting them. Willy now gave his consent, with the rejoinder that if Saglio wished to publish 'it is proof that this author has profited from my lessons'.

'This author', now an established mime, was back in Paris before *Les Vrilles de la vigne* appeared, dancing with Wague in a new mime-drama *La Chair*. She took rehearsals so seriously that Wague often teased her about arriving two hours too early for fear of being late or of not getting enough work done; though once she sent him a note: 'Dear friend, I'm not coming to rehearsal this morning. You won't get anything out of me in the mornings, because I can't go on rehearsing in the hygienic cloud of morning cleaners with trapezists over my head and whirring bicycles.'

Cover of first edition by G. Bonnet.

From 1907 to 1910 a great deal of her life was spent in hard work and discomfort on tour, dancing, and acting in *Claudine à Paris*, accompanied most of the time by Missy, who provided what comfort she could for her. 'When Missy is here,' she wrote to Hamel when she had a bad attack of 'flu whilst playing in Brussels, 'I can indulge in such luxuries.'

She sent a copy of the poster for *Claudine à Paris* designed by Sem to her mother. 'Sem', wrote Cocteau in *Portraits-souvenir* 'was a ferocious insect, ill-shaven and wrinkled, adopting, as he pursued them, the idiosyncrasies of his victims. Everything about him, his

Publicity poster by Sem.

figure, his round spectacles, his stub of pencil, his umbrella, his dwarf stable-boy outline, everything seemed to shrivel up into a concentrated desire to bite.' On receiving the poster Sido wrote to her daughter: '... it is very like you and he has even caught the way you hold yourself, that is, sticking out your left thigh, and pushing forward your pretty bosom. This is a criticism that I allow myself to make, and it's up to you to profit from it: to hold oneself well, one need only keep one's head straight between one's shoulders, and one's shoulders in the background, and that without stiffness or affectation.'

Sido was a harsh critic. She had seen Polaire play Claudine and told Colette that she did not like the interpretation, that Polaire brought to the role her own vulgar and coarse background. Polaire's success – seven years before Colette played it – was in any case phenomenal, but Colette's accent, this time far from being a detriment to her interpretation of a Burgundian girl, must in fact have added to her own undoubted success.

From Avignon where she was dancing in *La Chair* as well as playing Claudine, she wrote again to Hamel of Missy: 'Her presence makes everything easy.' In fact the tours were physically anything but easy: '... we get up at 5 am. Then an eight-hour train journey, play the same evening. ...' From Lyons: 'I wrote a postcard to you in the midst of confusion, hunger and tiredness, it must have seemed incoherent, this letter won't be any less so. I have an hour to myself before dinner and the opening night, and I'm grateful; I haven't had so much spare time since we began. The rest of the cast, used to touring and acting in a new play every few days, are terrible. We rehearse throughout the day, morning, afternoon and evening without complaining – it's good training, but hard. I can rest after this evening's opening, but my fellow actors begin rehearsing the next play tomorrow morning, and they do this for six months at a stretch! Honestly, I admire them.'

A chapter in *Belles Saisons* enlarges on this experience.

For a good tour, a really good tour, one needs. ... Yes, I know, one needs a well-known name, one that's up in lights – better still a star with a scandalous reputation. ... What are you talking about? For a good tour you need solid health, unshakeable good temper, nerves of iron, a well-disciplined stomach and bowels, and above all, that kind of optimistic nonchalance, that fatalism, which turns a touring company into pilgrims whose latent, sleepy faith rarely shows itself, but is nevertheless enough to lead it from place to place, towards the never-attained end ... towards rest. ... I'm not talking of stars, I mean those anonymous, humble people who tour all the year round ... pale from last night's train journey, bent from sleeping sitting up, who have three 'interesting, useful' roles in the same play: the valet in the 1st act, the guest in the 3rd, the doctor at the

COLETTE
WILLY

PUBLICITÉ WALL. 14. Rue LaFayette. PARIS.

dénouement; all those badly paid, ill-nourished unknowns, as they drag from town to town from one dubious-looking hotel to another.

For thirty-three days I led their life, that strange touring life, so special that it isolates you from everyone and everything; I've tasted its attraction, its bitterness, its fatigue and its disappointments. . . .

Claudine on tour was a great success, from the warmth of the audience and the box-office receipts to the critics' notices. Colette probably received the same payment as she did for her music-hall performances: 150 francs a day in Paris, or 200 francs on tour. Certainly she got no author's royalties; these went to Willy, Lugné-Poë and Valéry, who had adapted *Claudine* for the stage.

Touring in music-hall, in which dance-mime was only one of the items on the programme, had its own, different, difficulties. In Dijon the conductor of the orchestra totally ruined the first performance, and was subsequently discovered to be a local wine-merchant who had never conducted before. And there was the overwhelming heat of August in the Midi.

'Ninety-six in the shade, eh!'

And what will it rise to during this afternoon's matinée? How high will it be in my dressing-room, with its two windows, two right royal windows facing due south and shutterless?

After a dismal glance, devoid even of entreaty, at the panes set ablaze by the sun, I let my clothes drop off without any relief; my skin can no longer look forward to the biting little draught between door and window that only a month ago nipped my bare shoulders.

. . . A shrill note, a prolonged piercing cry, rises up to us from the depths of the theatre. This means that there really is at this very moment down there on the stage a rigidly corseted woman, who has achieved the miracle of smiling, singing, and reaching the gods with her high-pitched C, that makes my parched tongue thirst for slices of lemon, for unripe gooseberries, for all things acid, fresh and green.

. . . My cold cream is unrecognisable, reduced to cloudy oil that smells of petrol. A melted paste, the colour of rancid butter, is all that remains of my white grease-foundation. . . . Where can I hope to find the energy to move, walk, dance and mime?

Somehow or other, the mysterious forces of discipline and musical rhythm, together with an arrogant and childish desire to appear handsome, to appear strong, all combine to lead us on. To be truthful, we perform exactly as we always do. The prostrated public, invisible in the darkened auditorium, notices nothing that it should not, the short breaths that parch our lungs, the perspiration that soaks us and stains our silk costumes, the moustache of sweat and drying powder that so tactlessly gives me a virile upper lip. Nor must it notice the exhausted expression on its favourite comic's face, the wild glint in his eyes as though he were about to bite. Above all none must guess at the nervous repulsion that makes me shrink back at touching and feeling only damp hands, arms, cheeks or necks.

She was also deeply concerned about the sad life of the performing animals who, with acrobats, singers, show-girls and revue-sketch artistes, made up the rest of the performance. These animals had to suffer the same long train journeys, the same blinding footlights and airless dressing-rooms as the human performers. She tried not to become too involved in the misery of each, as she had no power to alleviate it, though once her compassion led her to buy the white greyhound bitch, Lola, whose thirst drew her timidly every evening into Colette's dressing-room for a drink of water denied her and the rest of the troupe by their Viennese lady manager. But she could do nothing for the tiny brown bear in the same miniature circus who seized his head between his paws, whimpering, every night, because a too-thin strap round his muzzle cut grievously into his lip.

Like the human performers some of these animals wilted, starved, and were over-driven; others took to the life with evident pleasure, like those actors who, in spite of earning scarcely enough to keep them alive, and however tiny their role, threw themselves into the work with the same boundless ardour as Colette. She herself not only experienced the mixture of attraction and misery of a touring actor's life, but also shared their dread of finding themselves out of work. Like them she was anxious about money, and in her letters to Wague about the payment they should receive for future engagements, as well as in her dealings with Charles Saglio about her writings, there is the awareness of the artist who knows that employment is intermittent and that he is totally dispensable.

At the beginning of 1908, soon after the appearance in *La Vie parisienne* of *Les Vrilles de la vigne* she started refurbishing the two novels *Minne* and *Les Egarements de Minne*, both of which had given her such pain, into the new version, titled *L'Ingénue libertine*. It was signed Colette Willy, and it appeared in the following April. The preface by Willy states: 'In common accord the authors of *Minne*, and *Les Egarements de Minne* have decided that a new version of these two volumes is necessary. This version in one volume having been entrusted to the sole care of Mme Colette Willy, the two collaborators have decided that she alone should sign it.'

This strange admission by Willy was the first indication that Colette had had any hand in that book, or in any other. Colette adds: 'In assuming the sole responsibility for this publication I am expressing an elementary scruple of literary honesty, by suppressing among a number of re-writes, that part of the earlier book which constituted the collaboration of the first signatory.'

She was firmly, and strongly, divorcing herself publicly from him as a writer. At the end of August 1909, whilst still touring both as

'Christine Kerf brought beauty, Colette originality, and I was the professional.' (Georges Wague)

actress and mime, she started writing her first full-length novel entirely uninfluenced by Willy's presence, and with total assurance relegated him to her past.

La Vagabonde is autobiographical in many ways: Willy appears in it under the name of Taillandier, the ex-husband, and the heroine, Renée Nérée, is a writer turned touring actress, whose experiences and thoughts are clearly Colette's own.

Renée is trying to free herself from love, from her enslavement to Taillandier; to wander free except for those bonds of affection between her and her touring partners and between her and her confidant, which make no demands. But she meets a rich, charming and uncomplicated young man, and though her spirit cries out against another subjection, her body leads her to the perils of falling in love once more. Finally, having separated from him for a few weeks, whilst she travels on daily early-morning trains to the towns where she dances each night, she manages for one moment to forget him.

How long had it lasted, that moment when for the first time I had forgotten Max? Yes, forgotten him, as though I had never known his gaze, nor the caress of his mouth, forgotten him as if the one dominating anxiety in my life were to search for words, words to express how yellow the sun is, how blue the sea, and how brilliant the salt like a fringe of white jet. Yes, forgotten him, as if the only urgent thing in the world were my desire to possess, through my eyes, the marvels of the earth.... You came to share my life. To share, yes: to *take your share!* To be a partner in everything I do, to insinuate yourself at every moment into the secret temple of my thoughts.... But I refuse to see the most beautiful countries of the earth shrunken in the amorous mirror of your eyes.

Though obviously a *roman à clef*, *La Vagabonde* is nevertheless a creative work built on rhythmic, almost symphonic lines, and shows Colette clearly as a writer whose phrasing, not only of sentences and paragraphs, but of the whole, can be compared to the work of a composer. She has said of herself that music came before words into her life. Newly heard music stimulated, even irritated, her nerves and brain, penetrated and haunted her, and played as big a part in her life from childhood onwards as in her brother Léo's. She would lie awake after a concert, her heels and jaws re-beating out the rhythms she had heard, trying to rid herself of them, resenting the invasion. Later she learned to let music enter her without resisting it. When she wrote she sometimes heard a sentence, the shape and the accents, before the actual words. 'A phrase of music or of language is born of the same evasive and immortal couple: sound and rhythm. To write instead of to compose is to follow the same quest, but in a less illuminated trance, and with smaller recompense. Had I

composed instead of writing I would have looked down on my métier of the last forty years; because words are stale, and the arabesques of music are eternally new.' Indeed, knowing the rhythm and sound of what she wanted to evoke she would hunt and chase a word until she had caught the exact and only one. Her language is individual, almost tactile, and absolutely unsoiled by previous usage.

I move my head imperceptibly because of his moustache which brushes against my nostrils with a scent of vanilla and honeyed tobacco. Oh! . . . suddenly my mouth, in spite of itself, lets itself be opened, opens of itself as irresistibly as a ripe plum splits in the sun. And once more is born that exacting pain that spreads from my lips all the way down my flanks to my knees, that swelling as of a wound that wants to open once more and over-flow – the voluptuous pleasure I had forgotten. . . . his mouth tastes of mine now, and has the faint scent of my powder. Experienced as it is, I can feel that it is trying to invent something new, to vary the caress still further. But already I am bold enough to indicate my preference for a long, drowsy kiss that is almost motionless – the slow crushing, one against the other, of two flowers in which nothing vibrates but the palpitation of two coupled pistils.

What seems to the reader to be a liquid flow of expression, a smooth and simple ease, was not in fact achieved without great difficulty. She found writing hard, as most authors and composers do whose work seems to flow so easily. She spent disciplined hours patiently waiting or diligently searching for the words that would most accurately express the moment, the colour, or the sensation she had caught and wished to transmit. Her books are concerned with discoveries rather than pre-arranged progressions; with intimacies sometimes expressed by seeming trivialities; but a description of a gesture, or a perfume can in a sentence reveal a whole person. The reader enters Colette's world in such flashes and inhabits it with her. It is a world of the senses, as surely as that child-hood world of the feel of the dust on the moth's back, the taste of early morning wild strawberries, and the purring of suckling cats. The themes of love, and freedom from love, which permeate the novels are made up of such daily minutiae of touch, taste, sound. Colette's senses were assailed daily, she was incapable of relegating into routine acceptance any sensation, however slight. The under-lying philosophies too are innate, and surprise by their lack of acquired thought. They spring from the untaught belief that neither the universe nor society is built hierarchically. And unlike most philosophers who only half believe in society's equality her credo could embrace not only the poor and the weak, but the rich and the downright silly.

The wholeness of her books,-their musical completeness, is often contradictorily not built in a progression of time. Even in her admittedly autobiographical works, in *Mes apprentissages* for instance, what she tells of her life with Willy is told as her memories come, not in order of days or years, but in revealing flashes, kaleido-scopically, each part building the edifice less expectedly but as surely as if she had started from the beginning and gone in an orderly manner to the end.

The genuine voice had been apparent as early as in *Claudine à l'école* when she was writing to order. The first time she had chosen a subject for herself and signed with her own name she had dared do something which might, in the climate of opinion in which she was living, have been embarrassing: she anthropomorphised animals to the point of writing dialogue for them. The work, though full of humour, is not fanciful in the sense of *imagining* the animals speaking a human language. It is rather an interpretation, a translation, of their thoughts and feelings.

Raoul Pouchon's rhyme, though amusing, accepts as did her other readers, her insight into the creatures' mentality.

> The language spoken by a beast
> Even if he be our pet
> We understand not in the least
> Unless of course we be Colette

What made *Dialogues de bêtes* acceptable, was simply that she 'became' the animals to the point of identification, and then inter-preted what she had become, in the same way as she became the human beings or fauns she depicted on stage; in the same way as she had felt one with the early mornings and the first rising bird of her childhood.

Whenever, in describing an animal's mood she puts words into its mouth, she is interpreting into language a bodily expression; she could, one feels, as easily have mimed it, that the language of her body could equally well interpret what the animal is feeling. When not on the stage, and given the necessity to interpret with words, she uses human speech to enable the reader to understand more closely what the body is expressing: the snake, knotted and coiled round its own barely visible head: '*Ouf! Je m'étouffe!*' The kitten cavort-ing, lost, in the gardens of the Palais-Royal: 'Help! I've been shut in outside!' The lost cat, following her, extricating itself, miaowing, from the crowds pouring out of the metro with her at Auteuil: 'At last, there you are!... What a long time you've been.... Where do you live? Go on, I'll follow you.'

In *La Vagabonde* she writes of the opposite transition: 'Nothing is real except making rhythm of one's thoughts and translating it into beautiful gestures.'

She has very occasionally in her letters or her reminiscences, shown glimpses of what the language of words meant to her; but these indications are a revelation of her whole artistic spirit as well as of her workmanship. In an essay 'La poésie que j'aime' in *Paysages et portraits*, she quotes a three and a half-year-old niece, who had recited, with an accent caught from her German governess, a poem she had made up herself:

> Here is zummer, very hotte
> And the sun shines like a beeg star
> And the moon she lightens us
> The whole night long.

Who can say how [Colette writes] by what miraculous grain, a childish spirit is self-sown with the seeds of poetry. It makes use of the far-fetched, of the incomprehensible, 'plastic' without thought, obtuse scansion, and of those deformed beats (offspring of rhyme and rhythm) that the child recites over and over again in secret, far from the opinions of adults and the judgement of reasonable people.

I am like the child (yes, a child again) who, silent and attentive for a long time in a train, came out of her silence to say: 'Oh, Maman, the train knows all my songs.'

At the start of life music and poetry walk with the same step. Then they separate. The musical refrain retreats, leaving the way and the precedence to the long pendulum of French poetry. The poem, the discovery of the poem, of its autonomous life, of its pulse which overrides our own, holds back or quickens our breath, what a momentous awakening in our existence. And that's only the first stage. Afterwards comes tardy curiosity, and amazement at the discovery that a poem trails behind it that obligatory load, its author. What! Those verses on a shelf in the paternal library, from which comes a smell of apples, and of mice, those verses are not the bequest of a thought, a snow-crystal, a parchment that belongs to nobody, one has to reckon with their author too! Oh, what a pity! But look, the author has a beautiful name and the title page shows us, engraved on steel, that the poet has an aristocratic profile and long fair hair ... it is thus, mesdemoiselles, you who are listening to me, it is thus that, in my day, I received, straight to the heart, the shock of de Musset.

In another context she writes

... for my part, to the best of my ability, I guard against the intrusion of involuntary verse – I track it down, I cheat it. You will tell me that this severity is overdone, that the ideal sentence is that in which each word is irreplaceable, whether the sentence is twelve or thirteen feet long. Leave me be, I know myself. If I didn't exercise on my prose a merciless control, I know very well that instead of an anxious and diligent prose writer, I would be nothing more than a bad, unleashed poetaster, and as happy in my metronomic universe as a tenor whose whole life has been nothing but a pure and interminable B flat! I am here. I am on the look-out. In some of my early novels, which date from my youth, there is some involuntary

versifying, not even camouflaged. As many as three lines one after the
other – I shan't tell you where. In one of the rare tête à têtes which I had
with the Comtesse de Noailles she told me that she couldn't understand
why I didn't attempt poetry. I replied that I didn't feel myself worthy.
And I asked her if she had never thought of publishing prose. She pushed
away such a thought with a gesture of her magnificent small hand. 'Never!'
she said, 'why should I use a language in which I couldn't say everything?'

In a letter to the actress Marguerite Moreno, her closest friend,
who, in imitating or describing something verbally, was unsurpas-
sably vivid, Colette writes:

You, who are magic itself when you recount something, you muff most
of your effect when you write.... 'A chorus of flatterers answered him' ...
'the conversation took a harsh turn' ... 'they began to judge him' ...
'mocking exclamations, derisory phrases'. Do you understand that in all
that no word *shows* me, or *makes me hear*, what you are talking about? ...
For God's sake no narrative! Touches, and detached colours; and there is
no need for a *conclusion*, I don't care whether you ask Proust's pardon, I
don't care if Sardou had been 'one of the kings of the contemporary
theatre'. Do you understand? ... 'a charming and delicate dinner' ... 'a
conversation that wanders from one subject to another', what does that
tell me? Give me a décor, the diners, and even the dishes, otherwise it
won't work. And try, o my dear heart, to hide the fact that writing bores
you stiff.

And in answer to Renée Hamon, who had written: 'But I don't
know what one should put in a book'. 'Neither do I, believe me. I
have only gathered a little light on what it is better to omit. Only
paint what you have seen. Look for a long time at what pleases you,
and for longer at that which hurts you. Try to be faithful to your
first impression. Don't believe in the "unusual word". Don't tire
yourself out by lying. Lies develop the imagination, and imagination
is the ruin of the reporter.... Beware of "embellishments", beware
of obtrusive poetry.'

At the time she wrote *La Vagabonde* she was already unwilling to
let anything pass until it had been refined to her own discerning
judgement. Her concern is evident in this letter to Charles Saglio
written in the February of 1910 from Grenoble where she was
dancing in *La Chair*.

It's not to annoy you, and it's not because of lack of confidence in
myself ... it's simply that I have just re-read what I have already written
of *La Vagabonde* and realise all that's missing in it, and all the changes I
must make, that I beg you instantly to stop it appearing in *La Vie* ... until
15 May.... I want to give you only a finished manuscript, worthy of you
as well as of myself ... I promise you a Vagabonde who will be there, and
not all over the place by the 15 May. You're not angry? ...

Samedi 21 Mai 1910

48ᵉ année, Nᵒ 21

LA VIE PARISIENNE

CONTES ET NOUVELLES
LES SPORTS

THÉATRE ET MUSIQUE
LES ARTS

PARIS ET DÉPARTEMENTS
Un an, 30 francs. Six mois, 16 francs. Trois mois, 8 fr. 50
ÉTRANGER (Union postale)
Un an, 36 francs. Six mois, 19 francs. Trois mois, 10 francs
LES ABONNEMENTS PARTENT DU 1ᵉʳ DE CHAQUE MOIS

PRIX DU NUMÉRO : FRANCE 60 cent. ; ÉTRANGER 75 cent.

RÉDACTION, ADMINISTRATION, PUBLICITÉ
20, boulevard des Capucines. Tél. : 148-59

DANS CE NUMÉRO COMMENCE :

Un nouveau   Roman

TOURN

LA VAGABONDE

par COLETTE WILLY

The young man in *La Vagabonde*, Max Duffein-Chautel, is said to be based on Auguste Hériot, who, rather than Missy, was her more constant companion at this time.

Colette had met Hériot one evening at Polaire's, during the time when he was Polaire's lover. An orphan, he was heir to the Galeries Lafayette millions. He used to entertain a variety of bizarre friends in his house, in a room where hung two near-priceless Gobelin tapestries of Fragonard nudes which he later sold to Pierpont Morgan for 1,500,000 francs (*d'or*). It was Hériot's pleasure and that of his friends to drink below the tapestry nudes and throw the dregs from their glasses upon the rare Savonnerie carpet at their feet. Hériot fell very much in love with Colette, but she evidently felt for him only compassion, motherliness, and a certain boredom.

Sidi

La Vagabonde was, as she had promised Saglio, ready for serialisation in *La Vie parisienne* by May, and by the end of 1910 whilst Colette and Hériot were in Naples – for once she was not on tour but on holiday – the book was entered for the Prix Goncourt. It obtained three votes in the first round, and Colette's hopes were raised. However, it was subsequently dropped, and the prize was won by Louis Pergaud with *De Goupil à Margot, histoires de bêtes*. Lucien Descaves admitted later: 'From the second round on, we only voted on books that we'd all read.' And André Billy, another member of the Académie Goncourt wrote as late as 1956: 'To have had the chance of crowning Guillaume Apollinaire or Colette, and to have missed it!'

Sido, who greatly admired *La Vagabonde* wrote to her: 'Minet-Chéri. You are not happy ... so little was needed for you to obtain the Prix Goncourt. You built your castles in Spain, and not without reason. Come! You must begin again.'

Nevertheless, *La Vagabonde* placed Colette among the top writers of the day. Because she had gained three votes from the Goncourt jury – as had Guillaume Apollinaire – she was, from now on, held in high esteem by the French *literati*; and Ollendorf published the book – as distinct from its serialisation in a magazine – early the following year, when it was not only well received critically but also proved popular. Yet the contributor to the English *Book of Writers* of 1913, Marie-Louise Fontaine, in a piece on French women writers, cited six contemporaries of whom only Lucie Delarue-Mardrus had written or was to write anything of note; and did not include Colette, who remained scarcely known in England, even as late as 1920, when both the *Times Literary Supplement* and the *Observer* gave *Chéri* unfavourable notices.

On her return from holidaying in Naples with Hériot, Colette began contributing a fortnightly column to the newspaper *Le Matin*, under the heading: 'Contes des Mille et un Matins'. She wrote at her choice, stories, music-hall anecdotes, pieces about animals, or events of the day. The commentary, or puff, which introduced her first article, stated: 'The story which *Le Matin* publishes today is signed only with an enigmatic mask. Behind this domino hides, by caprice, the identity of a woman of letters who is accounted one of the best writers of the day, whose very personal talent, made up of delicate sensitivity, sharp observation and youthful fantasy, has proved itself yet again with a new novel which is the success of the day.' The mask signature was kept up for four fortnightly columns, until on 27 February 1911 next to the mask was written 'C'est moi. Colette Willy'.

With her professional life as a novelist, journalist, actress, and dancer turning at top speed, her private life was gathering momentum into a whirlwind of equal excitement. Whilst she was dancing in Lausanne, Hériot went to stay with Missy in her villa in Rozven, Brittany, where Colette always went between engagements. Here Missy, strange unaccountable Missy, thinking he would be a good match for her friend, had prepared a conjugal room for the two. 'That in itself,' wrote Colette to Hamel, 'is enough to put me off him.' In any case Missy's move was untimely, because Colette had fallen in love with Henry de Jouvenel, the co-editor of *Le Matin*, and he with her.

Natalie Clifford-Barney found this relationship as unsuitable for Colette's earthy tastes as any of her previous ones. De Jouvenel was a man of immense sophistication who liked to entertain well, and who moved with ease in diplomatic and political circles. Colette herself described him as 'groomed, polished, trained in fencing and the use of words'. And certainly from his point of view Colette's way of life and some of her interests were surprising in the extreme: 'When I come into a room where you are alone with your animals,' he once said to her, 'I feel I am committing an indiscretion. You'll retire one day into the jungle.' His current mistress, Madame de Comminges, also seems to have had something of the jungle about her, as she was known as 'the Panther'. The week in which he left her and declared his love for Colette was one of tragi-comic proportions.

It began on 26 June 1911 when an unsigned piece was published in *Le Journal* which Henry de Jouvenel judged to be injurious to his newspaper. He immediately sent his seconds to the editor of *Le Journal*, challenging him to a duel. The editor, Letellier, refused to fight. On the following day, de Jouvenel published an open letter to his seconds Sauerwein and Joseph-Renaud, on the front page of *Le Matin*, which, referring to Letellier, contained these lines: '. . . the whole of Paris can wipe their hands on his face without any risk. When cowardice reaches such a point as we have seen today, it attains a kind of perfection.' In response, Letellier sent his seconds

ABOVE 'An artiste in her slightest gesture, with nothing of the intellectual about her.' (Sylvain Bonmariage in *Willy, Colette et moi*)

not to de Jouvenel, but to the proprietor of *Le Matin*, Maurice Bunau-Varilla, an authoritative little man, 'as tall as three apples', as Colette said of him.

De Jouvenel, insulted, forthwith sent his seconds to *those* seconds.

Finally, de Jouvenel fought with pistols in the Parc-des-Princes, against Georges Charlat, the features editor of *Le Journal*. Each wounded the other in the forearm at the first shot, and the duel was stopped. Colette's letter to Léon Hamel continues the story:

Did you know that the day after his duel he arrived in Lausanne* wounded in the arm, declaring that he neither could nor would live without me any longer? Do you know that at the same time H[ériot] wanted to join me in Switzerland and that I put him off with crazy, lying and contradictory telegrams? Do you know that when I got back to Paris J confessed to the P[anther] that he loved another woman? Whereupon she declares at once that she will kill that woman whoever she is. Distraught, J phones to warn me, and I reply 'I'm coming to see her.' And I went. And I say to the P 'I am the woman.' Whereupon she collapses at my feet and pleads with me. Short-lived weakness, because two days later she tells J that she is going to knife me.

* Where she was dancing in *La Chair*.

Re-distraught, J has me kidnapped by S[auerwein]; and S, J and I go by car to Rozven, where we find M[issy] icy and disgusted, having just heard the news from the P. Then my escort leaves and Paul Barlet stands guard, armed with a revolver. M, still icy and disgusted, bolts to Honfleur. Shortly after, J telephones me to come back to Paris, because the P is on the prowl looking for me, also armed with a revolver. So S whisks me back by car and here begins a period of semi-confinement in Paris where I am guarded like a precious shrine by the police and by J, S & S† those three pillars of *Le Matin*. And believe it or not, this period is only just over, terminated by an unexpected, providential and magnificent event. H and Madame la P have just embarked together on the yacht *Esmerald* for a six-week cruise having first startled Le Havre where the yacht was at anchor, with a drunken debauch. How do you like that? Is it good theatre? A bit overdone, don't you think?

At the end of the letter she writes: 'Need I tell you that I love that man, who is tender, jealous, unsociable and incurably honest.'

For the next few months, midst plumbers, painters, and mosaic-ists, they set about refurbishing de Jouvenel's house in Paris in the rue Cortambert, whilst she was dancing at the Ba-Ta-Clan, and he rarely got back from *Le Matin* before two or three in the morning.

† Sapène, also of *Le Matin*.

In August, she confessed in a letter to Christiane Mendelys, Georges Wague's wife, 'You want news of Missy? I haven't any, and she continues to keep all my possessions. I like exceptional treatment, and I shall be the first to benefit from "la Marquise" asking for money from a woman she has left. Sidi [one of her nicknames for Henry de Jouvenel] is on duty at *Le Matin* until the 1st and can only dine with me one day in four.' And in a postscript to a later letter to her, '. . . went to bed at 6.30 this morning after Gaîté – Rochechouart [where she was dancing *L'Oiseau de Nuit*]. We are as fresh and charming as a pair of the day before yesterday's fish!'

Nevertheless, by October, Colette had agreed to contribute a weekly instead of a fortnightly column to *Le Matin*. Her mother was censorious. 'So you are now going to write every week for *Le Matin*. I deplore it, because journalism is the death of a novelist, and detrimental to what concerns you. Look after your talent my darling; it is worth it.'

Colette in fact was no longer contributing short stories and anecdotes, she was now concerned with journalism proper, and had become a true reporter: using her extraordinary talent for words to evoke the essence of the day's events. Here are extracts from her report in *Le Matin* about a balloon ascent she made in September 1912:

Three hundred feet of cable are hanging down from the basket of the balloon at the moment, and beneath the free end of the cable there is still . . . brr . . . there is still over half a mile of empty space. . . . He looks at the lozenge-patterned shadow of the rope-net immediately beneath the taut belly of our golden bubble before saying: 'My friends, we shall have to land', then he throws out an opened newspaper which goes down, hovers motionless, then suddenly twists in frenzy, wheels round like a wounded seagull and falls. . . . Buzzing in our ears, near-enjoyable deafness, we're going down. 'Get down everyone! Cover your heads! . . .' Above us the flabby sides of the balloon shudder and struggle. . . . I see rushing towards us two venerable walnut-trees. . . .

The same year, she reported on being, albeit unwillingly, part of a mob:

'There's something over there . . . there's something over there on the right of the main road, something which everyone is looking at and nobody sees. . . .'

'Are they down there, the bandits?'

'Certainly they are, in that hut on the right. They're inside. So to stop them escaping again they're going to be blown up with dynamite.' They're over there, they're going to be blown up. This disgusting spectator-spirit takes hold of me, the same spirit which draws women to bullfights, boxing-matches and even to the foot of the guillotine. . . . Suddenly the wind brings us, along with the dust which gets between our

'The sides of the basket, I am assured, contain enough wine, sandwiches and chocolate to turn a landing on a desert island into a garden party.' (*Contes des Mille et un Matins*)

teeth, the obvious and startling smell of burning.... 'The house has been blown up. No, it's gun-fire, they're running away, they're running away ...!'

Nobody has seen or heard anything, but this nervous crowd which is hemming me in on all sides is inventing, unconsciously, by telepathy perhaps, everything that's going on over there. ...

People are shouting in confusion; the voices are hoarse and muffled like those of people sobbing. Shouting becomes clear, spreads, and the tumult turns into a rhythmic cry: 'Kill them! Kill them!'

'I'm pushed and bruised.... I must run at once if I don't want to be trampled underfoot.... I was a remnant of the crowd, oppressed and blind, I'm lucid again. I'm off in my turn to Paris, to find out what drama I've just attended.

In spite of Sido's fears, Colette was still writing, as distinct from reporting, though in fact there is very little difference in her own particular and individual approach, between the two forms. She wrote with the same awareness when reporting a moment of fear or a smell of fire as she did when she chose to describe one of the characters in her novels. Though Sido did not approve of many of Colette's activities, her disapproval stemmed from the very real and high admiration she had for her daughter's writing, and she was worried that Colette, with all her other interests, might not recognise just how precious a talent she had. For this reason too, she disapproved of Henry de Jouvenel.

'Ah! I'm not happy.' With pretended modesty I closed my eyes to retain the image of a handsome man, intelligent, envied, with a shining future, and I replied quietly: 'You are difficult.' 'No, I'm not happy ... I liked the other one better, the boy whom you now rate less than the dust.'

'Oh! maman! ... an idiot!'

'Yes, yes, an idiot ... exactly ... what wonderful things you would have written, Minet-Chéri, with the idiot.... The other.... You'll give him the most precious part of yourself. And you'll see, on top of all that, he'll make you unhappy ... that's more than likely.... Luckily, you're not in too much danger.' I understand now her 'You're not in danger'; ambiguity which alluded not only to my risk of calamity. In her eyes I had already passed what she called 'the worst thing in the life of a woman: the first man'. One only dies of the first man, after which married life, or its imitation, becomes a career.

Colette of course could not have chosen Sido's 'imbecile' as she called Auguste Hériot, because though her fear of domination was inbred, and to the men in those days incomprehensible, she had no desire either to dominate. She lived her own life in the innate and scarcely conscious belief in the equality of the sexes, though she never made the mistake of thinking of them as similar. They were rather, to her, beloved opponents. Neither in her actions, her letters, nor any of her writings does she uphold equality in any political sense. In fact she seems to have had no 'sense' of politics at all. In her journalistic assignments on political figures, and political events, it is always the person, the moment, she describes; never the ideological. Of Aristide Briand: 'A small hand at the end of a seemingly huge arm advances like an antenna.' Of Edouard Herriot's eyes: '. . . then begins that peculiar swinging movement from right to left, from left to right, that I have only seen in sheepdogs when, lying on the hearth, they *read* the interior of the fire.'

Henry de Jouvenel was in this respect Colette's opposite: a highly political man. He was also as different from Willy as any man could be. One of the first things Colette had noted about him was that he was 'incurably honest'. He was extremely handsome, not eighteen years older than she, but three years younger, a man of great brilliance and, as she found out very soon, of great courage. In his political attitudes he was a man of heart. Even before the 1914 war he was an advocate of trade-unionism, and a believer in European unity. After four years at the front he was to become a delegate to the League of Nations where he succeeded in getting his proposition for disarmament accepted by the forty-four member countries. By 1924 he would be Minister of Education in Poincaré's Government, then Minister of Overseas Affairs in Daladier's. High Commissioner in Syria, Ambassador to Italy, economist, historian, biographer . . . his talents were prodigious, and his integrity undoubted.

Colette's love was of course based on none of these admirable qualities – what she loved (and quarrelled with) was his childishness. Here is an extract from a letter to Hamel written not long after the event of the Panther and the revolver:

J. We must part.
C. Yes.
J. Life together . . .
C. . . . is impossible . . .
J. So, we are going to part.
C. At once.
J. Oh, there's no hurry . . .
C. I'm off to the rue La Fontaine.
J. That's unnecessary; and stupid. You are better off here.
C. No. Goodnight, Sidi.
J. But . . . where are you going?
C. Where I have things to do. You told me yourself . . .
J. Oh, what I said isn't of any importance. Wouldn't you like a game of bézique?

Within a month of that letter, after the couple had tried to separate, she was again writing to Hamel: 'Alas, I miss him terribly. His

presence ... his warmth, the sound of his voice, his vanity, his childishness and his ridiculousness. . . .' OPPOSITE Henry de Jouvenel, Editor of *Le Matin*.

In July 1912: 'There are good moments and wretched quarters of an hour.' In September: 'Rest assured, I am a pear bitten by the frost; you know that if it doesn't rot them, they become riper and sweeter-tasting, beneath their little scars, than other pears.'

In October de Jouvenel took her to Castel-Novel, the family seat in Corrèze. This enchanted towered castle surrounded by dense woodland is best described by Renaud de Jouvenel, who was a small boy at the time Colette first went there and was soon to become her stepson: 'Princess Marthe Bibesco called it "Leafy Castle"', he says, 'and Aragon "Rose Castle of Corrèze"'. For Renaud himself it belonged to a dream world:

The façade was eroded by wistaria and the back almost entirely covered with age-old ivy, which gave it a romantic aspect and for a child, that of a haunted castle. The interior was sad, even severe. . . . No electricity, no running water. Each evening, everyone provided himself with an oil lamp (which made shadows on the high walls) and we washed in hand-basins or zinc tubs. Water was brought up in huge barrels, by ox-carts from the farm.

'Everyone is charming to me,' Colette wrote to Hamel when she first arrived there, 'my mother-in-law as Sidi already calls her, is youth itself, and gaiety. There is Robert [Henry's brother], there is a young sister, a gentle giant of a child ... at 8 in the morning everyone is on the go; Sidi is at the farm, his mother at tennis. . . .'

And in December: 'Dear Hamel, we're getting married on the 19th at 4.30. But the registry office has to know your age!!!'

Sido was not alive to approve or censure the marriage; she had died three months previously.

Colette's first reaction to her death was torment that she would no longer be able to write to her. 'Sido – to whom I wrote two, three letters a week, full of news true and false ... of nothings, of me, of her – died in 1912. After twenty-three years, a reflex, that does not wish to die, sits me down ... at a hotel table if I'm travelling, and I ask for 'postcards with views of the countryside' ... and why stop writing to her? Why stop at an obstacle as futile and as vainly questioned as death?'

Sadly no letters or postcards remain, because Achille burnt them all when his mother died. He was himself to die only a year later, and also of cancer, aged fifty.

Colette could not bring herself to go to her mother's funeral. To her Sido was totally identified with that life-force, with those strong manifestations of nature which she herself paid tribute to all her life. She could not and would not associate her with death, with

Castel-Novel. 'The walls are alive with lizards, and yellow with bees.' (Letter to Léopold Marchand)

negation. Nor would she wear any outward sign of mourning. Sido's wishes, years before, had been wryly expressed: 'Don't let me ever see you in mourning for me! You know very well I only like you in pink, and certain blues.' But for some time after her death Colette experienced a painful internal inflammation, from which she had always suffered when she was deeply unhappy.

Because of her love for Sido she always felt that she had never appreciated her enough: '... bitches, their pups, cats, kittens by the dozen, the cow Violette, her calf who was taken away from her, the nightingales who, to pad their nest, intertwined soft chicken feathers with my long hairs, a mouse's litter, six baby mice fat as hornets, all sucking together their tiny mother. ... Did I notice my own mother less than all those mothers who surrounded me? It's possible. One doesn't notice the air one breathes.'

It was ten years before she began recalling her childhood and her mother, in *La Maison de Claudine* and another eight before she wrote in *La Naissance du jour*:

I am the daughter of a woman who in a poor, miserly and narrow-minded countryside, opened her village door to stray cats, to tramps, and to pregnant servants. I am the daughter of a woman, who in despair at not having enough money for other people, ran in the driving snow to cry from door to door at the houses of the rich, that a child had just been born in a penniless home, with no blanket, lying naked on feeble, destitute hands.... May I never forget that I am the daughter of a woman who crouched, wrinkles trembling, between the spikes of a cactus about to bring forth a flower, such a woman who never ceased to flower herself, indefatigable, for three quarters of a century. . . .

And two years after *La Naissance du jour*, in 1930, she wrote the culmination of her memories of her mother and her childhood in *Sido*, that short book which brings so vividly to life the woman whom even in her own old age Colette never ceased to celebrate and to learn from.

Sido in fact need not have worried that her daughter's talents would degenerate. Neither pregnancy, nor journalism – nor the difficulties of loving – could stem the flow of her talent. Within a few weeks of her marriage were published *L'Envers du music-hall*, *Prrou, Poucette et quelques autres*, and a few months later a full-length novel, *L'Entrave*.

The short *Prrou, Poucette et quelques autres* was printed in a limited edition of three hundred copies. On the title page of copy no. 62, printed specially for Gris-Gris, a Siamese cat, Colette had written: 'And for Raymond Poincaré: tender, cautious President Poincaré has spent sleepless nights because of Gris-Gris. "Who can guarantee," he once said to me, "that the railings round the gardens of the Presidency are not so wide as to let through the svelte and tawny body of the most loved cat in the world? The presidency is going to give me a great deal of anxiety."'

Of *L'Entrave* she later wrote: '*La Vie parisienne* which was publishing my book as a serial was beginning to catch up on me ... but in the contest between book and childbirth it was the book, thank God, that came off worse.'

Not only was she writing prodigiously, but continuing to dance, and her incredible energy kept her on stage until the seventh month of pregnancy: 'Euphoria, purring – what scientific or familiar name can one give to this grace? ... one grows weary of suppressing what one has never said, such as the state of pride, of banal magnificence which I savoured in ripening my fruit. Can I call pregnancy anything but a long holiday? One forgets the agony of the birth, one doesn't forget the unique long holiday.'

She did not want, nor did she attempt to describe that agony. Childbirth, like all pain, like illness, like old age, and like death, she neither wished to dwell on, nor to write about. Her labour took thirty unremitting hours. On 3 July 1913 she gave birth to a daughter, Colette, whom she called as her own father had affectionately called her in childhood, Bel-Gazou.

Her first reaction to her baby was to marvel, as she marvelled at everything else in nature, and in much the same way. 'Her nails, resembling in their transparency the convex scale of the pink shrimp. . . . The small sex, a barely incised almond, a bivalve precisely closed, lip to lip. . . .'

It was not until the baby was four months old and with a nurse in Castel-Novel, that she had to admit to her own surprise, that what she felt for the child was not only admiration but something she had feared she did not possess.

My God, how little one knows oneself [she wrote to Hamel] I arrive calmly, I find this little thing in the salon – and I burst into tears! It's probably quite natural, but I was surprised at myself. I find her so beautiful. She has an enchanting character, with outbursts of anger which give way at once and melt into smiles, and she has a reassuring gaiety. . . . She knows she possesses two ears, because when one has been cleaned, she proffers the other. She also holds out her hand, of her own accord, to go through a sleeve. . . . Sidi is mad about her!

Sidi was also getting up at six in the morning (this was November 1913) for an officer's training course, returning home 'voiceless and breathless' at 5.30 each evening after marching in mud all day.

Colette had spent the first two months of the baby's life finishing *L'Entrave*, which had already started its serialisation in *La Vie parisienne*, and desperately looking for a nurse. By sitting in agencies day after day she eventually found Miss Draper, a formidable English nanny of sergeant-major appearance, henceforth known to the family, evidently at her own suggestion, as 'Nursie-Dear'.

Nursie-Dear didn't believe in tears, and before the child was three had taught her that to be seen crying was as inadmissible as to do her 'business' with the lavatory door open.

How the child reacted to her upbringing is shown in two anecdotes: It is war-time. Bel-Gazou is four years old. The house is blacked-out.

I shall sit outside the room, my head against the door. Behind it, Bel-Gazou is already in bed. Nursie-Dear has taken away the one candle and is doing her evening chores before coming back. Bel-Gazou is allowed half-an-hour before she must go to sleep. And alone, in the dark room without a night-light she chirrups her imperious song of a nightingale in the shadows. English chatter, statements in dialect, interrupted songs, improvisations on a beloved theme, 'Come, Christmas, come', variations of fables, and 'Madelon, Madelon' and 'Where are you going to my pretty maid'. . . . The voice is dazzling, the tone varies from caressing to despotic; between words, between songs, there is laughter. . . . O silver cascades on white gravel, o rising fireworks that light up at the instant of falling, scales whose shrillest notes are a firebrand, grains of gold, sparks of crystal with a thousand reflections; there, behind that door, in that darkened room, my most treasured light: the voice, the laughter, of Bel-Gazou.

Colette and her daughter at Castel-Novel: 'Bel-Gazou knows that I admire her and that I won't tell her so.' (*Les Heures longues*)

The second incident took place a year later. Bel-Gazou had been in Paris with Colette, and was returning to Corrèze with her by train:

I leaned out of the window before the train stopped and I saw on the platform the tall, military back-view of Miss Draper. 'Darling! Bel-Gazou! Look, Miss Draper's waiting for us! Say goodmorning nicely to Miss!'

There was no question of saying goodmorning nicely! I had by my side, and so ravaged with emotion that she didn't think of getting out of the train, a little creature covered in tears which were rolling off her velvety cheeks without wetting them, and who was sobbing – 'Nursie-Dear ... ooh! Nursie-Dear ... Nursie. ...'

It was then that I learnt that a small child can cry for joy like a lover. As to Miss Draper ... I have never seen a military gentleman cry like that on a country station in full view of the guard. The next instant they had changed tack, and my daughter and her nurse had recovered their estimable dissimulation. My daughter described Paris with a grand air of disdain for the flower-covered meadow at her feet. Stiffly, Nursie-Dear repulsed the seductions she herself had not tasted. ... 'If you like your Paris so much, you should have stayed there. Me, I've been nice and quiet here without you to annoy me all the time.'

Nursie-Dear had spent those long years of war with her charge at Castel-Novel, digging the garden for their sustenance. 'How can I forget,' Colette wrote in *Paysages et portraits* 'that for the duration of the war a harsh, cross-grained grumbling foreigner, hard on others and on herself, exiled herself voluntarily into the country, alone with a small child, defended what I possessed, turned gardener, doctor, cook – and refused her wages.'

She wasn't in fact entirely alone. A thirteen-year-old local girl stayed with them, as maid to the nurse and the baby. Her name was Pauline, and she remained Colette's devoted friend, servant and constant companion until Colette's death forty years later in 1954.

Here and there throughout Colette's writings one notices the existence of servants; there was the washerwoman, and Henriette, from her childhood days; Marie who mopped up in Willy's flat after the hospital orderlies had carried out the bath when she was ill; a cook lent her by Marguerite Moreno in the 1920s for the holidays full of guests at Castel-Novel; and a chauffeur, Jacques, who had to go to hospital because he had an abscess. But she mentions servants not as menials, nor with any sense of social class, nor, with the exception of Pauline, as friends, but rather as equals whose job daily crossed her path, as the grocer's might or a neighbour's. Only in Paris during the early months of the First World War was she without a servant; in those days when she and Marguerite Moreno, Annie de Pène and Musidora lived partly together, partly as neighbours and shared the daily drudgeries of cleaning, cooking and laundering.

She recalls these times in her article on Marguerite Moreno which appeared in *Le Figaro littéraire* in 1948.

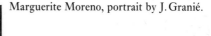
Marguerite Moreno, portrait by J. Granié.

... when the night sky was inhabited by zeppelins Musidora slept in my flat on a little iron bed, and during the day did the shopping, and cooked. I swept and laundered. ... Moreno sowed miraculous seeds of laughter, the nervous laughter of war, the insolence that stands up to approaching danger, witticisms as heady as a draught of alcohol. On windless nights, the hiccup of cannon-fire reached up, quite distinctly, from the east. It was enough to stop conversation, a disturbance both deep and intimate. ... One night Moreno, possessed by the rhythm of the cannonade, its strong and its weak beats, clicked her fingers and heels, and improvised on the spot a parody of a Spanish dance, and with the rotation of her hips and the rolling of her eyes, brought back our laughter, and made us unconscious of the danger, with the healthy impertinence and daring of a heroine.

War

HENRY DE JOUVENEL HAD JOINED UP on 2 August 1914, and was at the front from the very beginning of the war. He wrote from Verdun: 'The long queues of sobbing wives and mothers, the fathers who come and ask again and again for the bodies of their sons, which we cannot let them have, the letters from refugees who implore us to let them return to their village, even under bombardment, and to whom I have no authority to give permission, all this constitutes an appalling atmosphere. My dear love, you are still there, aren't you? You still love me? Fortunately there is that ... and Bel-Gazou.'

Colette meanwhile began night-duty in Paris at the Lycée Janson-de-Sailly, which had been turned into a military hospital. '... a terrible occupation, I'm not surprised that the work is not particularly sought after. Thirteen hours on duty, *every* kind of nursing duty, when morning comes one is somewhat haggard ... alas dear Hamel, it is sixty-four days since I have seen Sidi!' In *Les Heures longues* there is a chapter on this night-duty.

Sleep liberates the groans they have held back all day through pride ... the one whose eye and jaw are shattered says 'Oh!' from time to time in a shocked, scandalised tone of voice. That one, with the bandaged throat, is that a death-rattle? ... no, he's snoring, half-stifled.... From yesterday evening till now, they have only found crumbs of repose, broken, measured by fever, thirst, unbearable pain. They have begged one after the other for a glass of tea, of grog, hot milk, an injection, above all an injection....

She evidently felt the need, during those harrowing months, of having with her one of her beloved bitches as well as her delightful but intractable squirrel. In September she wrote to Hamel who was in Brittany:

If you come in October, would you be kind enough to bring Baghera and Ricotte with you? Of course I shall pay for Baghera's ticket (please keep her on the lead on a very tight collar). Ricotte should stay in her cage with some nuts and a few crusts, and you'll only have to give her some-

PREVIOUS PAGE 'Here I am ... in Verdun, under a false name, with borrowed papers.' (*Les Heures longues*)

thing to drink, a few times on the journey, from a glass or a cup, or even in the palm of your hand. I know I am asking you a great favour – but I really want them. . . . Sidi – well, he's fighting. I wrote and told him that I would love him to be here, and that *Le Matin*, God knows, constitutes an important part of his duties (it has had to stop publication during his absence), and he answered me with patriotic abuse. Can't you see him on horseback in the fumes? God is powerful who makes such soldiers. . . .

By the end of 1914, under a false name, with false papers and disguised as a nurse, she had succeeded, like other wives hiding in Verdun, in joining her husband. 'I guess at women, cloistered like myself behind persian blinds and darkened doors, their men, like mine, go off to their work with an air of indifference each morning. . . . Sidi is well, he seems as overjoyed that I am with him as I am . . . no-one talks of the war here, Hamel. We don't see the papers. . . . The only urgent question is the question of food.'

She hid in the house of a lieutenant and his wife whose home was in Verdun, accomplices who warned her not to go near the window because the army doctor opposite might see her. The windows shook with the force of the nearby cannons whilst the talk was of

Verdun 1915. 'They say they're really beginning to feel hungry in Germany and Austria.' (Letter to Léon Hamel)

finding butter, of a case of sardines that a piano-dealer had received, of the exorbitant price of turnips.

She remained near the front with her husband for some months, not without danger. Bombs shattered the windows of her bedroom. And once, when she took refuge with others under an iron bridge, a bomb fell in the water three yards from where they crouched.

De Jouvenel was a sub-lieutenant in the 44th battalion, and spent most of the four years of the war in the thick of the most appalling trench warfare. All the friends he made at the front were killed, or died of exposure at his side.

In the second year of the war Colette was sent by *Le Matin* (now back in circulation) to Venice and Rome as a reporter. Italy had just (July 1915) entered the war.

'I'm sick of basilicas,' she wrote to Hamel, 'and I detest St Peter's.' But the smaller churches, the fountains, and the gardens, enchanted her. It was already forbidden to go to Venice, but she persuaded the Chief of Police to give her a pass. 'Venice has kept only a whisper of her pre-war night life. A breathing that one can catch if one listens carefully: the lapping of a wave against a bridge, the creaking of a boat-chain, and towards dawn the discreet departure of a lone gondola.'

The immediacy of her reporting leads the reader to lean out of the hotel window with her, to see what she sees, hear what she hears: '. . . a second round of gun-fire, a third, further off. The magnificent echoes from the palaces reflect the sound on to the water.' . . . 'A peaceful crowd, noiseless, leans on the marble bridge; thin Venetians stretch their arms towards the aeroplane, the long black fringes of their shawls hanging like seaweed. . . .'

She spent the next two years between Italy and Paris, not only reporting, but writing a novel, *Mitsou*, and assisting at the filming of *La Vagabonde* in Italy, which was dropped half-way through because the film-company ran out of money. In mid-1917 de Jouvenel joined her in Rome where he was sent as French delegate to the Petite Entente; brief respite because by September he was again back in the front lines.

He and Colette were suffering from a 'poverty crisis'. Hoping to ameliorate their financial position, just before he returned to the front, she went by metro to deliver the *Mitsou* manuscript to a magazine – and lost it. As was usual with her, she had no rough copy, no notes, nothing. Sidi found her that evening in bed, her teeth chattering and a hot-water bottle at her feet, though it was a hot September night. But by the next morning she had recovered and began 'the most sickening task of my life ... redoing something already done'.

The following month Marcel Proust invited her to a small gathering in the Hotel Ritz where he lived during the war. She had not seen him since the salon days of Madame Arman de Caillavet, though they had corresponded and their admiration for each other's work was immense.

When I met him again, time and illness had worked upon him with haste. His agitation and his pallor seemed the result of a terrifying fortitude. In a frock coat in the centre of blacked-out Paris, in a timidly-lit hall, Marcel Proust welcomed me with a tottering gaiety. Over his suit he wore an open cloak. The sight of a crumpled white shirt front and a convulsive cravat frightened me as much as the charcoal smudges under his eyes and around his mouth, drawn there by distracted pain, blackening his face at random. The eagerness, the politeness he had always had, dogged his movements, his words, like the morbid traces of extreme youth. He offered a drink, a sweetmeat with the manners of a sixteen-year-old. Like many exceptionally fragile people, he became lively at the hour when healthy people admitted their tiredness.

At two o'clock in the morning as his guests departed, he stood at the entrance of the Hôtel Ritz: the silent night, the mist which blotted out the view, encircled Proust in a halo which suited his decline and his prestige. With his hat tilted back, a thick lock of hair covering his forehead, he looked, ceremonious and dishevelled, like a tipsy wedding guest....

As well as re-writing *Mitsou*, Colette was gathering together her war writings for publication, to help pay for furnishing the holiday house at Rozven in Brittany, which she and Sidi were hoping to occupy after the war. But peace was a long time in coming. In June 1918 in the worst part of the offensive Sidi was erroneously reported 'dead or taken prisoner', and as late as October 1918, after a five-day respite in Corrèze with Colette and Bel-Gazou, he was again back in the firing-line.

When the war finally ended and he returned, they lived for most of the year in the boulevard Suchet in Auteuil, and for the school holidays either in the little house in Rozven by the sea, or in Castel-Novel.

Apart from Bel-Gazou, de Jouvenel had two other children: Bertrand, fifteen years old, the son of his former wife Claire Boas, and Renaud, three years younger, his son by Isabelle de Comminges, 'the Panther' who had wanted to knife Colette. Both the boys spent most of their holidays with their father and his new family.

A snapshot [taken in 1920] groups the three offspring of different maternal beds ... catches them at a moment when they look almost tragically like themselves; the oldest in his worst imitation of de Musset, hair untamed, blond and salty, wild-eyed, charming, irresponsible and affected. The second – thirteen years old – enclosed, inward-looking, is a brutal little poet who would have died sooner than admit that he was un-

Rozven in Brittany ... to listen to the curlews calling as they fly by night.'
(*Paysages et portraits*)

happy and affectionate; and sooner than betray the least of his lyricisms. In this sturdy boy the pretty delicate nose, the fine, slightly receding chin, betray the mother's son. With them is to be seen my daughter, in all the bloom of her seven years, flourishing, impenetrable.

It is in Castel-Novel that Renaud remembers her most:

'Aunt Colette' had an immense bedroom on the second floor, with the biggest bed in the world, made to order, and upholstered in pink *toile de Jouy*, my father contenting himself with a smaller bed, covered in a material with greenish monkeys, illustrating the fables of La Fontaine. We used oil lamps, which threw disturbing shadows along the corridors, and left mysterious corners in the rooms. . . .

My step-sister Colette, nicknamed Bel-Gazou – (Beau Gazouillis?)* – with that musical and evocative shortening of words characteristic of her mother – and I were 'the children'. I can still hear 'Aunt Colette' calling 'Children!' at meal times, rather like one would call dogs, although they had the advantage over us. Their bran-mash was brought with deference, and with invitations to do it credit, whilst the children had to sit up at table, eat what they were given down to the last crumb and do what they were told to do, all of which was not required of the dogs. . . .

And Bertrand, the year of Colette's death in 1954, recalled those early days; this time at Rozven.

If you would know her, think of a garden in Brittany, by the sea. It is early morning and she has been awakened by the melancholy two-note whistling of those birds we call *courlis*; she has come down, carefully by-passing a small stack of sleeping cats, and the bulldog has followed her silently. She sits in delightful loneliness on the damp and salty grass and her hand enjoys the roughness of the herbs. The sound of the waves fills her mind, she looks now at them, now at the flowers which are moving faintly upward as the weight of the dew dissolves. From the still silent house will by and by emerge a husband weighed down with the cares of state, a bookish foster-son, a friend obsessed by the recapture of a lost lover, another whose mind is on the obtaining of a given professional position. Either selfishly or unselfishly their concern is with the world of men: to all of them, the newspaper, the mail, are a life-line to what matters. Not to Colette. She is completely unconscious of political events, wholly devoid of any ambition; indeed she is incapable of any planning or scheming in any realm, even to gain or retain any human affection. With those others she modestly disagrees as to who or what matters. What matters to her is the rapidly changing colour of the sky, the increasing roar of the incoming sea, the polish of a pebble which she had now picked up, and venturing further, the prompt dartings of a shrimp which feels that the tide will liberate it from its narrow pool. It is also the gait of her husband when he comes out: she will watch whether it is lightened by the enjoyment of the crisp air.

* Beautiful warbler.

The children were also welcome in the large town house in Paris, in the boulevard Suchet.

I had a strange dark room in the Chinese style then in vogue, with a divan-bed covered in black velvet [wrote Renaud]. In the salon downstairs which was equally dark, there was a piano which she played, and one of her canvases, because she painted as well as amusing herself sometimes with doing tapestry.... I remember seeing and hearing in the salon, the miaowing of a panther which someone gave her one day, and which my father took no pleasure in at all. There was also an unexpected squirrel, which jumped on my father's shoulders as he came out of the bathroom, which gave him a great fright, even though he'd just returned from the battle of Verdun; and there was even a snake which walked across the table during meals, but this seemingly did not stay long in the house. . . .

'Bertrand is splendid this year – as for my daughter, she's a love.' (Letter to Marguerite Moreno from Rozven, 1921)

Colette loved and cared for both her stepsons, and liked to gather her 'brood' as she called them around her: 'The Easter holidays will soon be here,' she wrote to Renaud at school. 'I would like to take all my nestlings to Castel-Novel, does that suit you? In spite of Easter being early perhaps the nightingales will sing? And the lilac make a small effort for us.'

'I think I can say,' Renaud wrote in the *Revue de Paris*, 'that she had a sincere affection for me, and that her letters to me were always friendly and understanding whereas my parents were often niggard with their affection. Her carnal, animal qualities, her lack of artifice, enabled her to communicate with me, abandoned child that I was, without pretence.'

Of his own mother the Comtesse Isabelle de Comminges, and her attitude to his father he writes: 'She certainly loved him, but in her own way, condescendingly: "You ride a horse so badly," she said, "you should really buy a buggy", and years later she asked me "Does your father still eat lamb-bones in his fingers?" and my father used to ask me "How's your mother?" as if he still felt the effects of her claws. I wish no-one such a mother; she was enough to traumatise any child, and for life.'

And of his father:

A proud look, an aquiline nose and undeniable presence; 'a dashing air' they used to call it. He had a fine tremolo timbre of voice which had a great effect on women and on senators, and he used it. He was quick-tempered and flew brusquely into terrifying rages. At heart he was tender, even weak, but hid his weakness under a crusty surface. No-one could deny his attraction, which brought him a great deal of good fortune, and for which I forgave him much. A veritable spendthrift, he nearly always led a sumptuous life. He has been compared to a Florentine seigneur of the Renaissance. To my mind he was also, above all perhaps, a Rastignac.*

To be his favourite son, which I was, and which all my friends confirm, was difficult, but had its compensations [he was] very secret, unable to confide in anyone. Bertrand cringed in front of him. Not I, who was as bad-tempered as he was.

All in all, he was an exceptional person, but he had no real friends; he made himself too feared.

And again of Colette:

She exaggerated. In some of her published letters, where she mentions me, I can hardly recognise myself. Because she overflowed with fantasy, saw people through a magnifying and deforming lens, she tended to idealise; she was carried away by the warmth of her temperament, her need to transform everything into literary material. She was naturally, sincerely, as exuberant in her writings as in her feelings. The succulence of her descriptions, the extraordinarily vivid perfection of her style – though very studied, as is proved by the numerous corrections in her

* Rastignac – a character in Balzac's *Père Goriot* – a social climber.

'Colette Willy – dancer and man of letters.'
(Sacha Guitry in *Comoedia*)

manuscripts – give a fair idea of her vivacity, of that kind of truculent vitality of the peasant, instinctive and full of appetite, which she never lost. . . .

At the time they fell in love, she must have looked very like the nymph lying on a velvet couch in the postcard reproduction captioned: 'Our Pretty Actresses: Madame Colette of the "Olympia"' and which was subtitled 'Total Offering'. The woman poses three-quarter face. Her hands form a cup (the offering), her elbows rest on the couch; her back is bare; her bottom and thighs are covered with a soft material alluringly draped; her feet are in the air; as for my father – whom she called Pasha or Sidi or both – he was of quite another race. An aristocrat, he never, as far as I know, relinquished his *hauteur* . . . but perhaps he had those repressed plebeian longings which my mother reproached him with. She was always ready to throw her genealogy at your head, never forgetting that the de Comminges had three centuries priority over the de Jouvenels . . . so he threw himself into the arms of a young odalisk who was above all intelligent, lively, cheerful, who knew how to love without making unreasonable demands, and showed in various ways an original nature, even though an extravagant one. I possess love letters from Colette to Henry de Jouvenel proving a love full of humility.

Nevertheless he states that in his father's circle Colette was regarded as a little stripteaseuse, and in his, Renaud's opinion, she was very pleased to have married 'above her station'. Colette might have been surprised by these attitudes had she known of them, since she never recognised that there was either a social hierarchy nor indeed one in the natural world.

When Colette was not occupied with the children, she concentrated chiefly on writing, but she was also acting, lecturing, visiting Algeria, and, being gregarious, inviting friends to stay and keeping up a correspondence with others.

When de Jouvenel was not busy editing his daily paper, he was immersed in politics, diplomatic missions, and social life. And fundamentally he and Colette were not in the least interested in each other's domain. From the end of the war until 1923, though living together, they followed the diverse activities of their very full lives. As well as practising politics he was writing political books, both of which activities seemed to him, very naturally, more worthwhile than those of his wife: 'Can't you write a book that is not about love or adultery or a semi-incestuous relationship, or a parting?' he asked her soon after the war. 'Isn't there anything else in life?' De Jouvenel was quite clearly expressing society's view of the artist, who has always been thought to be doing nothing; to be wasting time; to be immersed in a world which the rest of the world could very well do without. Of what *use* is art when poverty, war, injustice and other ills oppress the world of man? Of what *use* is it to

commune with words, with paint, with music? And yet, however much men of the moment work towards a better world for their fellow human beings, however devoted, tireless, revolutionary, they are in their doctrines, it is finally the artist who writes or paints our history, who offers us a better world, however temporary, through his music. 'Can't you write a book that it is not about love?' 'If he hadn't been in such a hurry,' she writes, 'for he was handsome and charming – to run towards one of his many amorous rendezvous, he could perhaps have taught me what could take the place, in or outside a novel, of love.'

Incorrigible, she sat down when he had gone out, and went on with her (to him) frivolous and useless work. She had begun *Chéri*.

This young man had started life some years earlier: 'Chéri? He was at first a little mongrel type, a bit crooked in one shoulder, with pinkish eyelashes and a weak right eye, who sniffed from a chronic cold in the head. With his air of a poor child, he nevertheless touched 15,000 francs a year pocket-money.... I must add that Chéri in those days was called Clouk, because of an unbearable little clucking noise he made in his catarrhy nostrils every time he drew breath.'

He was born, she says, of necessity, one day when she had great need of him for her weekly story for *Le Matin*. But one evening, when dining with his hard little mistress, Clouk saw at an adjoining table four mature ladies. Clouk 'caught a glimpse of his destiny, which was to die, and be re-born loved, that is to say, beautiful. . . .'

Feebly, as if I'd steeped him in a powerful soporific, Clouk lost consciousness, sank into nothingness and woke up in the arms of Léa, who called him 'Chéri'. I immediately made him twenty-five years old, dark-haired, pale-skinned, glossy as a six-months-old tom-cat. Sometimes I stood back to contemplate him. I never tired of beautifying him. His lashes, his hair like thrushes' feathers, his delicate hands, the curly hairs on his chest, and his teeth to be sure! And the curve of his lip . . . not knowing what further to heap upon him, I gave him this supreme gift: the majesty, the sense of honour, the childishness of a gigolo.

Chéri became like those young men of twenty, when Colette was in her forties, who having been lavished since birth with generous fortunes, now proceeded to lavish more and more on themselves: expensive cars, horses, yachts, furs, jewellery, were reserved for their own personal use. Colette also remembered a young man, the protégé of one of her mature friends. 'He wants everything,' the friend confided when the young man was out of the room, 'with one hand he swoops down on the foie-gras, and with the other he stuffs my famous emerald into his pocket ... and he knows nothing, nothing about anything.'

'When you are fifty you should write a sort of manual teaching women how to live in peace with the man they love.' (Henry de Jouvenel quoted in *La Naissance du jour*)

After she had created him she continued to see him among some of the young men she met: 'You do exist then? You really are as I described you?' And she admitted that he had, as they had, very little about them that was alive and human, except the melancholy of being physically perfect.

Twenty years after the publication of *Chéri* she wrote in the newspaper *Le Journal* that Chéri and Léa had begun life in her mind not as characters in a novel, but on the stage: 'I hesitated for a long time, watching the indistinct silhouettes of the mature woman and the too-young man emerge from the shadows. As they became more precise they exchanged those words, gestures, looks, which turn two lovers into two adversaries, and I wrote ... a third act, which, for want of a first and a second, I abandoned.'

Maurice Goudeket in a lecture, 'Colette et l'art d'écrire', given at Aix-en-Provence in 1959, said that Chéri was for Colette 'a chrysalis, representing her constant attempt to bridge the gulf between animals and humans; seeking obscurely to enter into human experience, groping towards the human warmth of a Léa, and inevitably falling back into his embryonic state'.

This kind of hidden symbolism, which can often be found in highly poetic works, as well as in children's art, is nearly always unconscious. The depths of his imagination which a great writer plumbs can seldom avoid symbolism. Any manifestation of nature becomes a part of the truth of the whole. 'Characters' imagined in depth become symbolic of their kind, though before the imaginative work we may not have recognised the 'kind' at all. All schoolgirls after Colette's first books could be seen, and saw themselves, as Claudines. It is part of Colette's genius that just as she identified with the characters she wrote, so legions of readers identified with what she had created. In the case of Chéri, though numbers of young men (and middle-aged women) identified with her characters, the symbolism which Goudeket discovers of the animal groping towards the world of humans lies at a different level of poetic imagination: a level which, though embedded in her understanding since childhood, did not surface in the book, but only groped its way blindly towards Chéri, just as he was groping. Colette herself saw Chéri differently, comparing his mainspring not with the young men of her day (that was a superficial aspect) nor with the animal world, but with music:

I shall no doubt be misunderstood if I say that for me Chéri has a symphonic value. His mutism expresses the disintegrating power of music, borrows disorder from instrumental, and more especially vocal timbres. ... The link between Chéri and music is less evident when Chéri sings out of tune. If he sang in tune his charm – using the term in the sorcerer's sense – would be explicable, even admissible. I do Chéri the honour of comparing him to music only because the latter is the delectable agent of all melancholy.

The serialisation of *Chéri* ran from 3 January 1920 to 5 June in *La Vie parisienne*. The week after it finished Colette wrote to her friend Lucie Saglio, wife of the proprietor and editor:

My dear Friend,

You are a 'chic type' and a perfect friend, and I am sorry I shall not after all be coming to see you this evening. I would certainly have come if I could have been sure not to encounter Saglio at your table. I have just received the letter in which he refuses to pay me the price he promised for *Chéri*. Having added 1500 francs to the 5000 he'd already paid, he considers himself quit. I only gave *Chéri* to Saglio because he boasted that he'd pay more than anyone else for it. I could accept that he'd only pay me *the same*, but I cannot tolerate this kind of slave-trading. Losing the money matters little; I'm worried that I shall lose you as a friend, and I don't want to lose you. Tell me you will remain my friend, and let us meet, soon, wherever you like. . . .

The critical reception of *Chéri*, typified by a piece in *Journal des débats* by Jean de Pierrefeu, surprised her:

Her art has always described uninteresting, vulgar and odd milieux which Colette herself seems to delight in. It is time she changed her characters. She has too much genius, surely, to degrade it in this way.

'But what is the matter with you, dear Pierrefeu, and others,' she wrote to him, 'that you should wish to alter me. To be drawn towards the pitiful – Léa, and Chéri even more than she, are the pitiful living among the pitiful – is that so base? I can't get that into my head, would you believe it? It seems to me that I've never written anything so moral as *Chéri*.'

She had sent a proof copy to Proust. It was two years since they had met at the Hôtel Ritz, and ill as he was, he replied:

As I do not know how long my lucidity will last, and as I can no longer see clearly having still not been able to get to an oculist, I am not certain that I shall be able to read the proofs of *Chéri* which you have been charming enough to send me before it appears in the shops. But yes. As soon as I have a couple of good hours I shall read them because the temptation is there, too near at hand.

You are too kind to want some Proust. The innumerable volumes of *A la recherche du temps perdu* are all written, right to the end. But that comes to the same thing as if they hadn't been. . . . You will receive a letter about *Chéri* which is certainly a thousand times better than my books. Anyway I have so much pleasure in walking about in your brain that I am not, at heart, displeased that you are not too bored in mine.

The following year he sent her a copy of *Du côté de Guermantes II* and *Sodome et Gomorrhe I*, with the dedication: 'To Madame la

Baronne de Jouvenel. Dear Madame, to think that I dared hope that we might one day be friends! I don't get up now that I can no longer see, and I have not even been able to go through the proofs of these, which have been printed from my uncorrected rough copy. How annoying to have seen you, and then only to know you as if we lived in two different epochs.'

For the past year Colette had been literary editor of *Le Matin* in which capacity she 'discovered' the young Georges Simenon. He had sent her some ghost stories and she wrote and asked him to come and see her. Her advice, which he later said was invaluable, was to cut out all the 'literary' stuff, and the beautiful-sounding adjectives.

'How pleased she seemed to have an American-type desk,' wrote Roger Martin du Gard, who had an office on the same floor, 'always covered in manuscripts and boxes of sweets. After searching under a pile of letters for her magnificent tortoiseshell glasses, which made her look like a young doctor in a comedy, she would gather together the galley-proofs of a story. She wrote, telephoned, sucked chocolates greedily, dictated, dealt out orders and laughter in all directions. Her hat in a corner served as a stable wreck among the torrent of books.'

Through her newspaper work she also became acquainted with the playwright Léopold Marchand, at that time a young man of twenty-nine. The first time she met him, only a few weeks after the publication of *Chéri*, with her usual forthrightness she asked him to collaborate with her in adapting it for the stage. This lack of caution, backed by intuition, was the start not only of a successful collaboration, but of a deeply affectionate bond. Though she was twenty years his senior they shared a sense of humour of the type to be found mostly among theatre people: they created for their own delectation, as can be seen in their letters to each other, mythical creatures called 'Gondins' and 'Khongs' who lived among puns and word-games. In their long association, although Colette very soon addressed him with the familiar 'tu', he never relinquished the respectful 'vous' with which he had first addressed the author he so deeply admired. Before he met her he had for himself alone and in secret started to adapt *La Vagabonde* for the stage. The attempt to turn it into a play, he later wrote to her, was 'a daily recompense, and also a call, a kind of prayer'. Her attitude to this kind of reverence was typical:

I overthrew the idols of this writer in love with literature. For the scenes that he wrote so reverently in such beautiful language, I substituted loose, rapid, malleable dialogue, the slack and living language that we speak in daily life ... such teaching bears fruit quite soon. If *Chéri* and *La Vaga-*

bonde owe a great deal to Léopold Marchand, my benevolent martyr who carries six foot above the ground his rosy baby-giant cheeks, his blonde waves, and the short-sightedness of his pink baby-elephant eyes – my victim learnt only one thing from me, but one thing which counts: the art of writing badly.

After seven months of working on *Chéri*, sometimes together, sometimes separately, Colette wrote from Castel-Novel to tell her collaborator that she'd finished it, that she'd re-written the end of the third act three times 'grumbling, swearing and profaning', that Chéri and Léa now talked right up to the final curtain instead of ending the play in silence, and that she had read the third act aloud to Sidi who was very moved by it. In the same letter she tells him that Bel-Gazou, now eight years old, has decided to marry a farmer, have four sons who will work on the land, whilst one daughter sweeps, another sews and the third cooks, 'and', adds Bel-Gazou, 'don't let anyone think I shall spoil them'. Also in the same letter, amongst the 'Gondins' and a reference to Marchand's fiancée, she writes: 'Do you know de Maupassant's description of England? "Too many tooth-brushes, and not enough bidets!"''

The play of *Chéri* opened in the December of 1921 at the Théâtre Michel in Paris, and a few months later, to celebrate its hundredth performance Colette herself played the part of Léa for one night. She played it many times in the following years, on tour. And once more the critics were divided:

No-one can replace her as a writer of remarkable books. Let her continue to write and leave acting to actresses.

... Don't let Madame Colette deceive herself; the audience only comes out of curiosity to see the writer in person.

... She does not act, she lives, she breathes, she fears, she conceals, she protects, she suffers.

Under a caricature in *Fantasia* of a huge matron in a red chemise holding in her arms a minuscule young man with a green complexion were the words: 'The character of Léa needs to be played by an elegant and beautiful woman, otherwise she is quite vile, inexcusable, and becomes simply a kept woman.'

Colette had indeed, from having been a slender young woman, become very fat, and at about this time was shocked to find that she weighed nearly thirteen stone. But so varied and prolific was her career that by the time these notices appeared she was already absorbed in a quite different subject. She had started work on the first of her books about her childhood. She was forty-eight. 'I am working like mad and shall probably die of it,' she wrote to Francis Carco; 'work is not my climate. But I have finished nearly eight

FOLLOWING PAGE 'Those who have not seen Colette play in *Chéri* have been deprived not only of an immense pleasure, but also of an understanding of this celebrated work.' (Gerard d'Houville [Marie de Régnier] in *Mercure de France*)

stories to date.' The stories were gathered under the title *La Maison de Claudine*. The title is odd, possibly the publishers – Ferenczi – thought that using the name 'Claudine' would add to its sales. Possibly Colette herself wished to wipe out the impression that Claudine's childhood was her own. She had always been totally identified with Claudine, even though it was believed that Willy wrote the books.

The *Claudines* of course were still selling, twenty years after they were written, and indeed are still selling. But *La Maison de Claudine* has nothing whatever to do with that heroine. It is made up of chapters of remembrance of Colette's own childhood, of her father, her brothers, her sister, and, most particularly, her mother. It is the first of the books of time remembered.

She was finishing writing it during the summer of 1922, at Rozven, as well as working on a stage adaptation of *La Vagabonde* with Léopold Marchand. She was also rewriting a novel, later to be called *Le Blé en herbe*. A few months earlier in the March of 1922 she had written to Léopold Marchand: 'I have lost my briefcase in a taxi with thirty pages of my next novel (I haven't one line of rough copy) as well as my weekly story for *Le Matin*.' For days she had haunted the lost property office, and advertised in newspapers; to no avail: the novel, then called *Le Seuil*, was lost, just as four years earlier she had lost the manuscript of *Mitsou* in the metro and had the 'sickening task' of re-writing.

And apart from all the writing commitments she had not only the three children to stay for the summer, but other visitors as well: 'Bring your copy of *La Vagabonde* with you,' she wrote when she invited Marchand, 'as naturally I have forgotten mine. Sidi-Zou-Robert-Germaine arrive tomorrow.'

Zou was Robert de Jouvenel's mistress, and Germaine Patat was at that period, quite openly, Henry's. She was a fashionable Parisian dressmaker, a great friend of Colette's and was to remain so even after the divorce.

Colette was never able to love two men 'concurrently' as she put it; de Jouvenel on the other hand could love – or at least have affairs with – more than one woman at a time; and Colette, though she declared that she never, even in old age, grew out of the passion of jealousy, never felt or showed antagonism towards her chosen female friends.

That summer she finished *La Maison de Claudine*, the adaptation of *La Vagabonde*, and was far enough advanced with *Le Blé en herbe* for the serialisation to start *Le Matin*.

It is an idyll of adolescent love, Phil is sixteen and Vinca is fifteen; and once more she had originally thought of it as a play. She had imagined an audience listening to a conversation about love, behind the curtain, and finding as the curtain rose that what they had heard had been spoken by two children. But she did not develop it as a play. As with Chéri, it seems that her characters were first of all imagined talking to each other, and this dialogue she heard as spoken aloud rather than saw it on the printed page. There is a lot of dialogue in her books, none of it flavoured by the author's voice, but bringing to life the rhythm and personality of the character.

But *Le Blé en herbe* had another setback. Once more the accusation of being shocking was levelled against her. The new literary editor of *Le Matin* stopped publication brusquely after the fifteenth chapter 'because of public protest'. However, she finished the book, 'not without torture', she wrote to Marguerite Moreno, for the publishers Flammarion. It was the first of her books to be published under the single name 'Colette', the signature she was to use for the rest of her life. 'The last page took me a whole day,' she wrote, 'and I defy you to believe it when you read it. What, these twenty lines in which there is neither fancy-work nor moulding – alas! that's how it is. It's the *proportion* that was so difficult. I so hate grandiloquent endings.'

Jean Larnac, her contemporary, writes in *Colette, sa vie, son oeuvre* that he finds in Phil and Vinca, Colette's philosophy of male and female. The girl endowed with an acute sensitivity, having a presentiment of things before the knowledge of them,* an individualist, anti-social; the boy, full of ponderous reason, obedient, hierarchical, obliged to learn everything in order to know it.

But Colette being a woman was not a philosopher in that she held a theory and demonstrated it. She could not be theoretical; she wrote what she sensed, and if a philosophy emerged it was because her senses were true. Throughout her books there is indeed this opposition of the male and female, their mutual incomprehension, and their resultant solitude in the presence of each other.

Early in 1923 the adaptation of *La Vagabonde* opened at the Théâtre de la Renaissance in Paris. In an interview with the newspaper *Comoedia* after the opening she said: 'To my mind, as the situation in a play mounts, as it becomes more violent, so the language, to compensate, must subside. When one's in a passion one doesn't choose measured words, correct expressions. I personally would find it impossible.' It was fourteen years since she had written her ideas about dialogue in the *Comoedia Illustré* and she had evidently not changed them: 'The modern theatre,' she now said, 'must in my opinion forbid itself pompous speeches in the classic style'. Marchand in an interview with *Le Capitole* said that he would write a few pages of the play based on the characters in the book

---

* *pressentant les choses avant de les savoir.*

and send them to her. 'Soon afterwards she'd give them back. Nothing seemed changed: exits, entrances, stage business, silences, all there. And yet, nothing was left except the imperfect framework where new beings moved.'

When some time later Colette herself played in *La Vagabonde*, André Rouveyre wrote: 'She speaks rather quickly and in a manner frankly detached from her partners, as if she were saying: "If you think it amuses me acting with these puppets."'

But André Rouveyre was accustomed to sacrifice truth to wit, both in his writings (in which he never became very successful) and in his caricatures, for which he was justifiably famous. He had always slated Colette on stage, from the 'flat thud' of her dancing, and 'the audience only comes out of curiosity' in his notice of *Chéri*, to his adverse criticism of her as Renée Nérée.

A month after the opening of *La Vagabonde* in Paris, Colette was once more on tour as Léa in *Chéri*. De Jouvenel was also away a great deal, on diplomatic missions. They were growing further and further apart. The tour over, she wrote to Marguerite Moreno from Castel-Novel in October that Sidi had sent her on ahead from Paris saying he would join her the next day, but had not turned up. 'Amour, amour,' she wrote, 'anagram of amour? Rouma. Add "nia" and you will find a lady with the bones of a horse, who lays two-volume books' (to which Claude Pichois, editor of the letters adds the 'discreet' footnote: 'this indication will permit readers to recognise her'). The apparently unmentionable lady was the Princess Marthe Bibesco. 'And now,' writes Colette, 'I wait for him from one hour to the next, one week to the next. . . .'

Renaud de Jouvenel believes that Henry's mother, 'Mamita' as he calls her, very much wished for a permanent liaison between her son and the Princess:

Did she play a part in the divorce? [he writes] I don't know, but it's possible because she had an overwhelming love for her son Henry . . . and liked to interfere in other people's affairs. And it is unlikely that she would have appreciated Colette's rather uncouth manners. Her letters prove that she was delighted to welcome my father home when he left – rather abruptly it is said – the town house in the boulevard Suchet. . . . Germaine Patat didn't please her . . . she had her own candidate, the Princess Marthe Bibesco . . . and if she'd been given the slightest occasion to disturb the Henry-Colette set-up, she would certainly not have let it pass.

But whatever the relationship between the Princess and Henry de Jouvenel, it was Germaine Patat who 'triumphed' as he puts it.

A week after the 'Roumania' letter Colette wrote again to Marguerite Moreno: 'Sidi will be here on Sunday. . . . Having with difficulty given birth to thirty pages for my lecture on 'The Problem of Living à Deux', I realise that I mustn't at this moment touch on the subject, for a number of reasons.'

Instead she decided, for her lecture tour, to speak on animals, on rejuvenation, and on 'On Either Side of the Footlights'. 'I speak on stages – like Aix and Avignon – which are icy, in a perishing tempera-ture at which animals and flowers can no longer exist.'

In *L'Etoile Vesper* she remembers 'at La Rochelle the obscure alley sign-posted 'Artistes' Entrance' straddled a black streamlet and led into a glacial hall', and at Cannes, 'in hail and ice, I struggled against fever, decked with cupping-glasses, sitting on four injections of camphorated oil. . . .'

She returned in the December of 1923. The following month she wrote to Wague's wife, Christiane Mendelys, consoling her for having been deserted by her husband, and in a p.s. added: 'I have been alone for a month. He left without a word whilst I was on a conference tour. I am divorcing.'

Natalie Clifford Barney had evidently foreseen that the marriage could not last. In her *Souvenirs indiscrets* she writes: 'It was not without apprehension that I saw Colette, married to Henry de Jouvenel, installed valiantly and lovingly in a real house with a handsome husband, a baby, a nanny, servants, etc; in spite of their shared tastes in food and sex. . . . In any case how could this tall dark man at the peak of his prime, intelligent and vain, who pleased women so much and was so pleased by them – remain with one woman only?'

Rumourmongers had it however that de Jouvenel was divorcing Colette – for infidelity with his son Bertrand. They assured each other that Colette was Léa and that Bertrand was the model for Chéri conveniently forgetting that the book had been written four years before, when Bertrand was only fifteen. 'The drama of the divorce would be delicate to evoke if Colette hadn't described it with too much detail in *Chéri*,' writes Willy's old friend Sylvain Bon-mariage, who on his own admission had hated her since the day he had asked her to make love and she had refused. 'Léa is Colette and Chéri is Hippolyte,' he goes on. 'Racine shows us Phèdre tormented by a culpable love which is not incest. There is no blood relationship between Phèdre and Hippolyte. He is only the son of the first marriage of her husband. Nothing, absolutely nothing is con-summated. Boulevard Suchet is another kettle of fish: Jouvenel was suddenly and fortuitously the ocular and auricular witness. Nothing could stop the separation. It was only a question of avoiding the scandal.'

What part of Bonmariage's imagination invented 'the ocular and auricular witness' it is hard to guess, and he gives no clue to back up the statement. Perhaps he did not know that Colette had been away alone for a month on tour before coming home to find that de Jouvenel had left her. Certainly he would not have had access to her letter to Marguerite Moreno: 'All alone, with neither a cast nor a director, and alone to unpack and re-pack my luggage daily, and take another train . . .', written from Marseilles on 23 November, nor her letter to Léopold Marchand on 14 December: '. . . if you have anything urgent, I have left the dates (and approximate addresses) with Bertrand, who lodges at 284 bd Saint-Germain'; nor her letter to Charles Saglio at the end of December after her return: 'I am battling against my unhappiness as strongly as I can, don't worry. My friends – and you are one – help me. The children too, the three of them.'

Before and during this period, her letters to Marguerite Moreno with whom she had always exchanged the most intimate confidences, give not the slightest hint of a relationship with Bertrand – far from it – though she was always maternally concerned about his health. In 1921 (when he was seventeen): 'Bertrand is fine this year, and he swims like an eel. Renaud swims too . . . as for my daughter she is like a little dolphin in the waves.' 1922: 'If you could see Sidi-Neptune surrounded by his little tritons, Bertrand, Renaud, Colette, and his large triton – me. . . .' May 1923: 'Everyone here greets you, Sidi, Bertrand and even Pati [the Brabançonne bitch].'

From the affectionate tone of her letters to Renaud, whom she called 'Kid', she seems to have felt much more for him than she did for Henry's elder son; and Renaud admits that at the time he knew nothing about a relationship, though later he repeated the rumour: 'People believed Bertrand was the model for Chéri.'

But his chief reason for believing otherwise himself was his knowledge that Bertrand was terrified of his father: 'Utterly impossible that he would have done anything to provoke his anger – absolutely impossible – he had no courage.'

As for his being the model for Chéri the first stories about Chéri appeared in *Le Matin* in the January, February and April of 1912, ten months before Colette married de Jouvenel, when Bertrand (whom it is unlikely she would have met at that time) was exactly eight years old.

The divorce in any case was arranged quickly and without publicity by de Jouvenel and his friend Anatole de Monzie, a friend of Colette as well as of de Jouvenel, who not long after became Minister of Finance, and later Minister of Education.

Very soon after the divorce Colette decided that she must cease to write for *Le Matin*; the situation was indeed too difficult for her to continue; but she did not relinquish journalism, and from now on wrote regularly for *Le Figaro*, *Le Quotidien*, *L'Eclair* and others. But for a year after the separation she was cast down, depressed, and less resilient than she had been for a long time. Her letters to Marguerite Moreno reflect her mood. When de Jouvenel's brother, Robert, died that July she wrote: 'Alas, it was the *only* great and deep affection of Henry's life.' And later in the same letter: 'Yesterday I saw Monzie. His faithful Ramie [his secretary] told me that the day before yesterday Monzie had said to him "I get the impression that Henry regrets having disorganised his whole life."'

The little Colette at boarding-school was suffering too from the separation, and was continually in the sanatorium. 'They tell me at the school "She'll be ready to travel on Saturday, come and fetch her and take her to the seaside. She needs it, formative years, insecurity etc." … I'm working, but badly.… I've had to produce three articles in the last few days – I could have given birth more easily to three pairs of twins, I believe.… I have such a horror of work that I have sent a telegram to the *Figaro*. "Ill. Article FOLLOWS NEXT WEEK." … I am heavy with an incredible torpor.'

She was attempting to write not only articles, but books. In March she wrote from Montreux to Francis Carco: 'I came away to work on one novel, and of course I'm working on a different one.… It's terrible to think, as I do every time I start a book, that I no longer have – that I never had – any talent. …'

But by the end of 1924 she had recovered something of her *joie de vivre*, and was playing Léa at Monte Carlo with a cast not of actors (this was the idea of the Théâtre-Casino) but of authors, all of whom took their acting very seriously and in fine amateur tradition. Jacques Deval counted the words of the part of Desmond offered to him, and turned it down because it was too small. Léopold Marchand dared not refuse the small part of Patron, but glowered malevolently at a professional actor who had a larger part, and consoled himself by buying an expensive suit, special shoes, boxing-gloves, and a purple cap for his ten-minute appearance. As for Tristan Bernard – he slipped away from the stage between two of his cues to place a bet on one of the gaming tables.

The following year she played in the Paris revival, this time with a highly professional cast, which included Marguerite Moreno as Chéri's mother.

She had also, after many years of setbacks, succeeded in bringing to the stage an opera for which she had written the libretto. The project had been first mooted before the war, early in 1914, when Jacques Rouche the director of the Paris Opera House commissioned her to write one, and asked Ravel to compose the music, though, he admitted, 'that could take a long time'. Colette's libretto was titled

Divertissement pour ma fille until the day Ravel said to her with icy seriousness: 'But I have no daughter.' Having accepted to do the music it was not until five years later, in 1919, that he wrote to her suggesting she develop the squirrel's song, and asking her what she thought of making the cup and the tea-pot into black Wedgwood figures singing a rag-time. Colette was delighted with the idea: 'May a terrifying gust of music-hall blow through the dust of the Opera House!' Her patience lasted *another* five years, then she wrote to him 'Oh! dear friend, when, when . . .?' And in 1925, 'Henri de Roths-child will take the opera for the opening of his new theatre . . . on 1 March. . . .' In fact the Théâtre Pigalle was not ready until the following year, and the opera, now re-titled *L'Enfant et les sortilèges*, had its première at Monte Carlo on 21 March 1925 and was not played till a year later in Paris, at the Opéra-Comique, when it had a very mixed reception. Colette wrote to her now thirteen-year-old daughter '. . . it plays twice a week to full but hostile houses. The partisans of classical music can't forgive the composer, Ravel, his vocal and instrumental daring. The moderns applaud and howl down the others, and during the miaowing duet there's a terrible uproar.' A defence of the piece appeared in the magazine *Le Théâtre et Comoedia Illustré* a month after the opera opened: 'Every per-formance has given rise to both hostile and enthusiastic demonstra-tions . . . is it really necessary for a management to receive unanimous approval, that it should stick to works by composers whom the public no longer allows itself to question? The talent of Maurice Ravel is nevertheless no more in doubt than that of Monet or Renoir.'

Paradise Regained

A MONTH AFTER THE MONTE CARLO OPENING of the opera in April 1925 Colette was invited by Marguerite Moreno to dine with her at the home of some friends. Also invited that night was a more frequent guest, Maurice Goudeket. '... as I entered the drawing-room I saw Colette there ... she was lying flat on her stomach on a sofa, dressed in a print frock. With her head raised under its crown of dishevelled hair, and her bare arms, whose beautiful modelling at the shoulders struck me as being a bit too plump, she looked like a large cat stretching itself. I had never met her, never heard that bronze voice of hers, rolling its Burgundian Rs. Why it was I do not know but I observed her without charity.'

'I thought that evening,' Goudeket once said, 'like a great many people did when they first met her, that she was playing at being Colette. But after living with her for thirty years I came to the conclusion that she must indeed *be* Colette.'

They did not meet again for another month, and then Colette's first letters about him to Marguerite Moreno give a taste of the beginning of that happiness she and Goudeket found in each other, that was to last right up to her death. 'Ah! la la, and again la la! And never enough la la! Your friend is in beautiful hot water up to her eyes, to her lips, and to further! Oh! how devilish calm people are – I say that of young Maurice. Would you like to know what young Maurice is like? He's a rotter and a this and a that and even a *chic type* with a skin of satin. That's how deep in it I am....'

Twenty years later, when she was seventy-two, she wrote in *Belles saisons* of the friends who visited her, '"We heard you laughing" they'd say, "as we came up the stairs ... what was it about?" And we'd answer: "Nothing. It's just that he was with me, and I was with him."'

Goudeket out of a natural delicacy never asked her about the past. He felt it would be a trespass. And unlike her other husbands he had no desire to change her. He was thirty-five when they met – she was fifty-two. He had, of course, like thousands of others of his genera-

PREVIOUS PAGE Drawing by André Dunoyer de Segonzac at La Treille muscate.

158

tion in France, read her works when he was adolescent. 'My infatuation was no recent thing. I was fifteen or sixteen years old when I
discovered Colette, and received from that first reading of her a
delicious shock.' His contemporary Thierry Maulnier, remembering his own adolescent thrill on first reading Colette, wrote that the
other great authors he was discovering introduced him to new
worlds; Colette introduced him to his own.

At the time of his meeting with Colette, Goudeket had contributed
a number of articles to various magazines and was also (although he
never found a business career very satisfactory to his romantic and
literary turn of mind) a dealer in pearls. At the beginning of the 1914
war, when he was twenty-four, he had joined the French foreign
legion, and been twice decorated. As a stranger, he had sent her
some of his war poems, published in 1917.

He writes of himself:

I had never learned how to pass from a madly imaginative childhood, fed
by literature, to a more realistic youth and maturity. . . . By the time I was
thirty-five I had still not sobered down much, so in order not to betray
this childish state of mind I behaved with the greatest circumspection
which made me appear cold and formal, not quite at ease. When I did
occasionally form an attachment I would break it off at once, because I
wanted to keep myself with all my emotions intact for that unique love in
which, at the bottom of my heart, I no longer believed.

Soon after they met he introduced her to Provence in summer-
time. It was totally different from the Brittany she knew and from
the Monts-Boucons of her Willy days, but she fell in love with it as
she had with the other parts of the French countryside, and before
going off on a tour of *Chéri* she looked for a cottage to buy. She found
one in Saint-Tropez called 'Tamaris-les-Pins' which she considered
a nice name for a railway station, and before buying the property,
renamed it 'La Treille muscate'.

I found it set back from a road avoided by cars, and behind the most
banal railings – railings suffocated with oleander, in a hurry to offer
passers-by through the bars, powdered bouquets of Provençal dust, white
as flour, finer than pollen. . . . Two hectares of vine, orange-trees, green
figs, black figs – When I say that garlic, pimentoes and aubergine abound
between the vine-shoots and the furrows, have I not said everything?
There is also a house – small, low – but of less account than its terrace
covered with wistaria for example, or than its red-flamed bignonia or the
old thick-trunked mimosa, which, planted from the railings to the terrace,
pays the house hommage . . . do not ask me where I shall plant the white
rose blown down by the wind, the yellow rose that smells of fine cigar, the
pink rose that smells of rose, the continually dying red rose whose dry,
light corpse still lavishes its balm of incense. . . .

Before moving into her new summer home she continued to write the book she had begun some months before, as early as December of the previous year: the sequel to *Chéri*. 'I'm working on my novel with a despairing courage,' she wrote to Marguerite Moreno. And by mid-September of 1925: 'The end of Chéri will be my own end, it——s me so much. But I'm working madly.' From time to time she had to stop writing to go on tour with *Chéri* but she refused all newspaper work until she had finished it. 'It will be a rather gloomy book,' she wrote, 'and totally bare. No rare word, no decoration. I have taken a dislike to ornament which surprises even me.' And at midnight on 22 October: 'I *must* finish *La Fin de Chéri* now. My God, it's difficult. I have 240 handwritten pages. That's a lot. But it's not all. If I don't write to you it's because I'm working hard, and disconsolately.'

At the end of the year she walked into the office of her literary editor at Flammarion, Max Fischer. 'When she was writing,' he said, 'she usually seemed more tormented and nervous than usual. That afternoon, she came into my office smiling, and seeming very pleased with herself. "Well, Colette, can I ask you for news of Chéri: I don't know why but I think it must be good." "Good!" exclaimed Colette gaily, "it's excellent! Everything has gone well. . . . I'm rid of him; I've just killed him off."'

But she was less happy on the day of publication. The extraordinary ill-chance that dogged her work from time to time – the signing of her books by another, losses in metros and taxis, the stopping of publications, the truncating of serials – now played its unkindest trick. On the morning of publication a friend telephoned her to tell her what had happened, and Goudeket saw her turn pale. *La Fin de Chéri* had been published with thirty-two printed pages omitted. So that not only did the non-sequitur between pages 156 and 157 make total nonsense, but a great deal of the rest of the book became unintelligible.

Colette telephoned her publishers at once to tell them what had happened, thinking that perhaps it was only the first few copies, and was horrified to discover that the whole first edition of 35,000 books had already gone out.

How could such a thing have happened? Goudeket suggests that Colette may have overlooked the omission; but this explanation is not in character. It is more likely to have been a binder's error since each printed section of a book is quite often of thirty-two pages.

She took a long time to get over this appalling mischance. Her precision, her rhythm, her careful attention to detail and to character were thus nullified, and the effect must have been of an author who did not care.

Goudeket writes in *Près de Colette*: 'For any writer worthy of the name a book is the product of a slow and painful exudation into which each time he puts the best of himself. During a year or more the work has been re-read, corrected, weighed, taken up again, re-written. When it finally appears, the author is in such a state of anxious expectation that the smallest misprint is enough to throw him into despair, and a forgotten word can torture him. Imagine when it is a chapter.'

Perhaps there was something in her nature which courted such mishaps. Her meticulousness had always been devoted to the details of her work – the finding of an exact word, the describing of an elusive moment, the chasing of an evocative memory – rather than to the appurtenances and outward shows of authorship.

Though as a child she had been intrigued by her father's desk with its white paper, its rulers and rubbers, its paperweights and pens, none of which ever moved him to write a word but were loved for their own sakes, Colette herself never needed more than the edge of the desk that Willy allotted her, a post-office pen and school exercise books. Though these needs changed they never got any grander – nor any more meticulously arranged – either in her news-paper office or in her work-room in any of her houses. That she could leave a manuscript in a train or a taxi was quite under-standable, since her thoughts at the time were probably centred on the characters in those manuscripts and not on the briefcase which contained them. Her creative mind thrived on disorder around her, and harmony within.

La Fin de Chéri, published six years after *Chéri*, is the continuation of Chéri's story after the 1914 war, when a 'naughty boy's' beautiful eyelashes and the pervading perfume of a cocotte no longer had any meaning. The world of the first book, though it was written as late as 1920, dealt with an earlier period; a period of *poules de luxe,* a society of lavished, kept, young men; a world of restaurants, of dressmakers, of gossip and the races, of luxuriant henna-ed hair piled under huge hats, and of rose-coloured bedrooms.

In the second book, Chéri returns to Paris after the war to find not the land fit for heroes which he and his fellow-soldiers had been promised by the Government and the newspapers, but a world of total disillusionment. His friend Desmond who had evaded call-up is now rich and callous; and his own mother, and his wife Edmée (though they have been doing hospital work) have made fortunes out of clever investments in cotton when they realised the over-whelming need for bandages.

Edmée refuses to have a child by Chéri. 'Another you? No thank you, once in a lifetime is enough' sets the seal on the past. Chéri's one hope is to find his Léa, his 'Nounoune' who represents for him his youth, his lost paradise; the mother-figure, the incorrupt.

This wish of Chéri's to return to purity was shared by Colette herself. She continually refreshed herself from the pain of loving, of disillusion, of the corrupting influence of city life, by returning to the source of her joy, the earth.

She exorcised her suffering either by retiring to the country-side or by remembering and writing down what it was she had lost.

I will tell you the names of all my dead cats and dogs, I will annotate for you the funeral chant of the two fir-trees; that miaowing in a minor key that rocked me to sleep; and the young high-pitched and gentle voice of my mother, calling my name in the garden. . . . You will hear my shy owl hoot, and the heat of the low wall, decorated with snails where I used to lean, will warm your arms crossed one over the other and . . . quick! Close your hand! Close your hand quickly upon the hot and dry little elusive lizard. . . . Ah! you shivered! You were caught in my dream, then?

Thierry Maulnier believes that this land of childhood which is also the land of return, is an inviolable sanctuary, the heart's centre, and is by its essence that which cannot be shared even with the most beloved. But of course Colette does share it, even whilst guarding its inner sanctum she offers it to us, because it is the core of her life, and a great writer writes from that alone.

The heroines of her novels, like herself, retire from the shock of an unhappy affair or marriage, to regenerate themselves among the flowers and the woods, where they find the peace and strength to begin again. Thus Claudine in a letter to Annie: 'Armed only with a deep regret and a small valise, I went back to my native soil. To die? To recover? I didn't know which when I left. The divine solitude, the pacifying trees, the blue and counselling night, the peace of the wild animals, turned me away from an irreparable intent, and led me gently back to the country from which I came – to happiness.'

But unlike Colette and her heroines, Chéri, returning to Léa after seven years' absence, fails to re-find his earthly paradise in the fat, jolly, rather masculine Father Christmas of a woman that she has become. Behind the grey, shingled hair and the avuncular voice he is unable to discern what *was*, that which memory had preserved for him intact. Horrified, he leaves her with a banal excuse, goes back to the airless room lent him by a drug-addict, and shoots himself.

'With Colette,' Goudeket writes, 'the happenings of her life had no influence whatever on the tone of her books. . . . *La Fin de Chéri*, a hard, bitter book, without a smile, was composed at a time when she had reason to feel unreservedly happy.'

Colette was not only happy because she was once again in love – but for the first time it was love without the turbulence and buffeting of quarrels and incompatibilities. For the first time this complete and individual woman was not asked to change to suit her mate. The Pygmalions who had tried to shape her nearer to their desires, who had fallen in love with what they supposed was raw material for their imagined perfection, had not only ignored the fact that she was as rootedly herself as she had been as a child ('You used to be rather set in your ways, morally and physically'), but that that self could be something to respect and nurture in its own individual mould. To their chagrin they could not remould her, though Willy could temporarily destroy her, and Henry de Jouvenel, like many of her other critics, could advise her to write about things that did not interest her; advice contrary or irrelevant to her purposes.

But now Colette in her maturity had met a man who for the next thirty years cherished her not for what she might have been or might yet be, but for what she was. Goudeket had never before totally allowed himself to love with his entire nature, Colette had done so to her cost. That first summer in Saint-Tropez was for her, unbelievably, at fifty-two, a paradise regained.

Is this my last house? [she wrote of La Treille muscate] I take its pulse, I listen to it, while that brief interior night which follows the mid-day hour, slips away. The cicadas and the new wattling which shades the terrace, creak and crackle. Some other insect crunches small chippings between the shell-like elytrons of its wings, the reddish bird in the pine-tree calls every ten seconds, and the considerate west wind which circles my walls leaves in peace the flat dense sea, strong and rigidly blue, which will soften towards day's end. Is this my last house, the one which will find me faithful, the one I shall not abandon? It is such an ordinary house that it can know no rival. I can hear the clink of bottles being replenished for this evening's dinner. One wine, gooseberry pink, will accompany the green melon. The other, amber-coloured warm and gritty, goes with the salad, tomatoes, pimentoes and onions steeped in oil, and with ripe fruits. After dinner we must not forget to irrigate the channels which surround the melons, and to water the garden balsam, the phlox, the dahlias and the young mandarin trees whose roots are not yet long enough to drink from the depths of the earth, nor have yet the strength to become verdant without help, under the constant heat of the sky. Young mandarin trees. Planted for whom? I don't know. Perhaps for me.

In the ten o'clock night air, blue as convolvulus, the cats will snatch at moths, with vertical leaps. The two drowsy Japanese hens will chirp as in a nest, roosting against the arm of a garden chair. The dogs, already retired from the world, will be thinking of the approaching dawn, and I shall have the choice between book, bed, and the coast road lined with fluting toads. Have I recaptured here that which one never recaptures? Everything resembles the first years of my life, and I recognise little by little, in the confines of the rural home, in the cats, in the aged bitch, in the wonder, the serenity whose gentle breath I sense from afar – merciful refreshment, promise of healing rain hanging over my still stormy life – I recognise the way back.

'A spoilt dog is a calculating liar, a cat is deceitful and secretive. Bâ-Tou hid nothing.' (*La Maison de Claudine*)

Remembering Bijou, Nonoche, and the chaplet of suckling kittens in the house at Saint-Sauveur, it is not surprising to find that there were never less than ten cats living in La Treille muscate, excluding the caretaker's cats, the local toms who came to call, and the friends' cats boarded out with Colette whilst their owners went on holiday. There was Mini-mini ('because she hasn't got a name'), Kro, Kapok, Muscat, La Touteu, Petiteu, Pichinette, Minionne, Toune; and of course, La Chatte, La Dernière Chatte, the One and Only, the female Chartreuse whom both Colette and Goudeket loved as their child.

And, among the dogs, a new and most beloved French bulldog bitch, Souci: 'Imagine!' she wrote to Marguerite Moreno, 'I have a bulldog bitch. Sixteen months, brindle, marvellous in every way,

first prize in the show. I bought her quietly without telling Maurice beforehand. Having studied the marvel, and lamented the price, I made a resolution.' The resolution was to cancel the brick wall she had ordered to protect the vines from the lower road, and buy the bitch instead. 'She is called Souci. . . . At 10.30 on Sunday morning she came for a walk with Pati [the Brabançonne bitch] and me, *and I did not put her lead on for one moment.* That was a test, for both of us. She sleeps with Pati and all is well. I confess, my dear one, that I get great pleasure from this charming companion. Don't scold me.'

Her proximity to Souci, in all senses, is deliciously evoked in her *Journal à rebours.*

I am only dozing, it is siesta time, but Souci sleeps. She sleeps in the bulldog manner, that is to say she is all tremors, running in her dreams,

her jowls shuddering, trying to escape, to bark, perhaps to speak. In the depths of her imaginings her eyelids open, but her large brown eyes see nothing but the inner drama of sleep. My cheek, close to her flank, feels the unequal up and down of her breathing, and the disordered beatings of her heart, five little beats, rapid as the toc-toc toc-toc-toc of the death-watch beetle, haunter of old woodwork. Then a single 'toc' hanging between two interminable silences – a single one, the last? . . . No, just when I myself, having caught the affliction, was about to suffocate, three mad palpitations follow. . . . Such is the normal course of a bulldog's heart.

It was in the summer of 1926 that Colette had packed up everything in the house at Rozven, to move to Saint-Tropez. Pauline was away on holiday, but the young Colette, at thirteen, was as strong and able as her mother, and they managed it between them. No doubt the child was delighted to have her mother to herself for a change, and it is evident that they took a great deal of pleasure in each other's company. Colette's feelings towards her daughter were those of admiration, of camaraderie and of delight in her looks. From the moment of the young Colette's birth she was aware of the miracle but admitted that at first 'I did not feel the meticulous admiration I devoted to my daughter as love'. Certainly she said at a later date that of all creatures she had a preference for cats and for her own child; and it seems that whenever she wrote about her, whether in recording incidents in her books, or writing of her in letters to her

La Chatte and her kitten Jantille.

La Chatte at five months.

167

friends, she not only admired and cherished her, but felt a genuine maternal love for her. And yet she was so totally unpossessive of her that she could, and did, go for long periods without seeing her. And though this may have been responsible for the admirable independence of the child, it also led to a lack of intimacy between them – a feeling on the child's part that it was a bonus to be with her mother, to whom she always showed the most sincere and the most loving side of her nature.

Colette had believed that leaving the child to be brought up by Nursie-Dear was the most responsible thing – under the circumstances of the war – that she could do. Nursie-Dear was a disciplinarian, and Colette admired and even relished discipline. Her strict attitude towards her own writing and dancing, and her description of training Souci, as well as her letters to her daughter at boarding-school, amply bear this out.

But however much she admired the English nanny's firmness she must have been somewhat dismayed when Bertrand reported to her on holiday in Rozven, when the child Colette was six or seven years old, that Nursie-Dear not only often locked her up as punishment, but also beat her. (Renaud remembers her as a 'nasty old witch who hated me as much as I hated her'.) The nanny's strictness, however, was confined to punishment for misdemeanour and to discouraging self-indulgence. She evidently wished to impart to her charge the prevalent English proclivity for the stiff upper lip. But she did not limit her physical freedom. On the contrary she allowed the child to run freely in the countryside all day, pursuing her unknown pleasures without any adult supervision. As a result when young Colette eventually had to conform to the rules of a French boarding-school, she could not manage it. She was expelled from the two schools she attended in France, first in Saint-Germain-en-Laye, then in Versailles.

She herself, at eight years old had asked, in her confident and independent way, to be sent to boarding-school when Nursie-Dear left, and Colette had agreed; but when, not long afterwards, her parents' marriage broke up, the child's confidence deserted her, and she felt lost and abandoned. From then onwards during the holidays she had to stay with one parent or the other, never again with both, and she missed the family unity which she remembered chiefly as 'meal-times full of laughter'.

Colette, absorbed in her own difficulties, had not taken the child's reactions into account and was surprised when, on returning to stay with her alone for those first holidays, she said to her mother 'I want to be Jewish. May I ?' Colette looked at the child with the same interest that Sido might have given a flowering cactus and asked

Renaud de Jouvenel, Bel-Gazou and Nursie-Dear.

'Why?' The child explained that Jewish parents loved their children and often came to school to visit them. She evidently felt unloved and became difficult. When, a few years later, she broke one of the school rules and was in consequence not allowed home for the week-end, Colette's respect for discipline and for human dignity was apparent in the letter she wrote to her: '... you are disposed to treat your teachers lightly, and also your class-mates. You sense in your-self a little demon who, from the height of your thirteen years, judges, appreciates, esteems, condemns. You sin, my darling, by such audacity. (It's enjoyable – it's dangerous.) I could easily have fallen into the sin of self-satisfaction, I who was brought up in a village school, surrounded by little peasants slow of understanding. A kind of scruple preserved me from believing myself superior, from thinking of myself as a swan among geese.'

The letter has echoes of Sido. However painful it must have been to receive, it is the kind of salutary advice that can only come from a loving mother who appreciates her child's intelligence and under-standing.

But though she had the security of a mother willing and able to guide her through her difficulties, there remained, for the child Colette, the lack of a stable background. The long summer holidays were spent partly with Colette, partly with her father in Corrèze, or with one or other of their friends. Thus the holidays were split up going from one person to another with the attendant discomfort of travel-sickness.

Between the two French boarding-schools, she attended at twelve years old an English one, in Bristol, where she seems to have fitted in better than in the over-rigidly disciplined French ones; at all events she stayed there for six months, and was not expelled.

But the effect of having a famous writer for a mother was naturally inhibiting for the daughter, however warm their relationship, and however unimposing the mother. By the time she was fifteen she stopped writing letters to her. 'But why?' asked Colette. The girl replied that anything she wrote would seem stupid. 'Darling,' Colette replied, 'witty letters are addressed to strangers, not to one's nearest.' And certainly none of Colette's letters to her friends show any sign of being composed for publication, nor for any eyes but the one person she is writing to: 'Wait while I change my pen' – or on paper torn out of an exercise book, writing with a cold in her nose to Marguerite Moreno: 'Ba Barguerite.'

Writing a book was not a free and easy occupation, but a pain-fully difficult one. Towards the end of working on *La Naissance du jour* she wrote to her daughter to congratulate her on having passed a typing exam: 'I am just emerging from a nightmare of work, part of

En route for school in Bristol. Colette de Jouvenel aged twelve with her father at Victoria Station.

it too difficult and which takes away my sleep. Two more difficult days and I should be working with a less heavy heart. That's a hope, not a certainty.'

Young Colette too had a heavy heart. Her father had insisted that she learn typing and dressmaking on leaving school, both of which occupations she thoroughly loathed. But he believed in women working. A year later, at sixteen, she got work as a secretary, and not long afterwards in a *maison de couture*, which gave her for the future a rooted distaste for buying clothes. Her talents lay in quite different directions, but she would be seventeen before one of them was put to the test.

In the maturity of her happiness Colette was still pouring out her energies in writing novels, touring, changing house in Paris, visiting Spain and Tangiers, and doing dramatic criticism for *La Revue de Paris*. And although *La Naissance du jour* written at Saint-Tropez in 1927 incorporates in its mixture of fact, fiction, past and present a 'portrait' of Colette as a woman who has renounced physical love, this was in fact a vision of the future. Colette in her fifties was more physically and more happily physically in love than she had been as a young woman. She does not bring Goudeket into the book. Though people at the time supposed that Vial was Goudeket, the character was in fact a mixture of fiction and a young antique dealer acquaintance. She never used Goudeket as a character, as she used Willy and Auguste Hériot in *La Vagabonde* and possibly Henry de Jouvenel in *Julie de Carneilhan*. He was to her complete without the aid of written words, and she was far from any need to exorcise him in print. He appears only in her last diary-like writings as himself, tenderly enquiring if she is not bored as she lies bedridden on what she called her 'raft'.

Vial, and the other fictitious character, Hélène, are not of prime interest in *La Naissance du jour* nor are the lesser characters, her friends in real life, André Dunoyer de Segonzac and Luc-Albert Moreau, painters who worked as early and as hard in the fields as any peasant farmers, and whose women made up the entourage of her summer friends. The magic of the book lies in its evocation of time and place, of thought and memory, of plant and animal, of Sido and of the present day, and of the woman living there surrounded by her past and her present, digging in the garden, walking the coast road, content among her animals.

In a passage evoking her mother in old age, she recognises the very essence of what was important to them both: '... she got up early, then earlier ... trying to possess the beginning of the beginning. I know what that particular intoxication is like ... she wanted the damp wing that the first bee stretches out like an arm; the scent of acacia and wood-smoke blown by the summer breeze before the sun is up; her reflection on an autumn morning in the first disc of ephemeral ice on the bucket of well-water. . . .'

André Dunoyer de Segonzac who illustrated *La Treille muscate* and also painted a portrait of her, wrote of those St Tropez days on the occasion of her eightieth birthday for *Le Figaro littéraire*:

. . . Colette called her cats; as the Muslim calls the faithful to prayer, so Colette called her animals for a walk. 'The Cat's Walk!' This recitative, scanned musically, made the cats asleep at the top of the mulberry tree decide to come down from the tall trunk on the tips of their long claws; they followed Colette in procession along the alleys bordered with purslane and amaryllis. . . . I waited for her in the downstairs room where she worked every day. She wrote at a small Provençal desk, which she had placed in an angle of the room, so that the two walls isolated her like blinkers: a voluntary prisoner. Before starting work she *had* to delay, as Claudine might prolong the recreation period; she lay on the divan with her pug bitch, then squatting on the stone floor, she de-flea'd her bulldog bitch Souci. Then followed a pitiless attack on flies. Then, quite suddenly and resolutely, she sat down to write. Her beautiful strong arms leaned across the desk. She stayed there, stiff with an immobility which lasted several hours; she remained completely absorbed, said not a word, in absolute calm. Only the crumpling of a page of text, which she threw away with a contained rage, broke from time to time the total silence. Brusquely, around dinner-time, she got up and said: 'That's enough of that for today.' She called Maurice, draped a cape around herself, and departed surrounded by her animals to join her friends at the port.

For all her camaraderie and love of friends, another of her neighbours, Paul Géraldy, who later in 1937 adapted her novel *Duo* for the stage, spoke of her innate shyness: 'If you talk to her of her work,' he said, 'she calls one of her cats and scolds it. It's her defence.' Her defence, perhaps, against knowing the effect of her work. Praise is always more difficult for an artist to combat than criticism, because the praise may hit upon something which the artist does not want consciously to know about. As an actress Colette knew what every actor knows – that if someone told her how well she did a particular action, she would not be able spontaneously to do it again. She would have been shown it from the outside, not from the thought that produced it and in consequence it would in future lack life. Colette's need to defend herself against praise of her writing may well have been for the same reason; the fear of stopping up the source of her work by knowing too clearly what its outward appearance was. She had always instinctively evaded the taint of self-consciousness. She was still the same woman who had shied from Willy's wish to advertise and to be seen, the same woman as the child pursuing her early morning questing, unwilling to be watched. There is a fine distinction between the opening of oneself to the waiting page or the theatre boards where one can still commune, unharmed, with discovery; 'protected from the whole world by a barrier of light' and the talking about or seeing what one is doing through another's eyes. The degree of conscious, semi-conscious or sub-conscious work necessary depends on the individual artist, and whether the work is beginning or near completion.

When she was writing [says Maurice Goudeket in *Près de Colette*] she used sometimes to concentrate so hard that she would gradually get colder and colder. She put rug after rug on her knees and shawl after shawl on her back. When she was finishing a book her application became such that one had the impression she was really giving of her substance, as a bee gives its honey. Capable at such times of working eight or ten hours at a stretch, she used in the end to look like a cocoon. Whether she liked it or not she was not far at such times from a sort of trance-like state.

On her love of words he writes: 'She even loved certain words for themselves, quite apart from the idea which they represent. She loved them for their music but still more for their graphic aspect, their design. Has she not spoken somewhere of the letter S "standing on end like a protecting serpent"?' And at seventy she herself wrote that the pleasure of doing tapestry work was heightened by 'the thrill of an extraordinary majestic M girdled with roses, a number 2 sitting up and begging, a Q resting on its tail'.

'During periods of intense work,' says Goudeket, 'she would dream of words. "I've had a typographical dream," she sometimes said to me in the morning. Words and lines had danced a ballet specially composed for her. When a journalist from *Le Figaro* asked her if she was in favour of simplified spelling, she answered: "I don't want to have my words spoiled."'

This appreciation of the rhythm and shape of words and letters is evident in the text she wrote for a limited edition of lithographs by Matisse: *Dance Movements*. 'Except for the first, they have scarcely any face, nor do they need any, leg in the air, leg on the ground, head lost, an arm here, an arm there, she falls, she collapses, she yields – up to a certain point. This certain point is the hand, the vigilant mind, of the painter who fixes it, and who from a disorderly body, draws the promise of an eternal equilibrium.'

Her sense of equilibrium was all too often unbalanced by editors and publishers; those people who held the power to present or withhold her work from the public. Their decisions were beyond her control, and final. As an instance, in the December of 1928 at the request of Pierre Brisson, whose mother, Yvonne de Sarcey, was the director of *Les Annales*, she sent her new novel *La Seconde* for serialisation. Having accepted it, he later asked for alterations. 'You

At La Treille muscate – etching by André Dunoyer de Segonzac.

fear that the readers of *Les Annales* may be, for reasons founded or unfounded, scandalised,' she wrote to him. 'I think not, but you are the sole judge of that. I have made the cuts you ask for. From the literary point of view I have done wrong. From friendship, I have behaved according to my feelings.' And she adds that she will take the manuscript back rather than submit to further cuts. Again, in 1931, Bunau-Varella, one-time owner of *Le Matin*, asked for her next book *Ces Plaisirs* ... for serial publication in *Gringoire*. She sent it to him. But after the fourth week he wrote to tell her he was stopping publication because he'd had a number of protesting letters. 'He told me in a short note,' she wrote to Germaine Patat, 'that he was going to make cuts and that if I didn't wish to do them myself, his staff writers could. I gave them permission, and as you can see they have cut it in the middle of a sentence!' Indeed, after the half-finished sentence, in large type was printed the word FIN.

In this book, later retitled *Le Pur et l'impur*, she writes of the homosexual and lesbian societies she has known and frequented; of the young men who gathered in her room in the rue de Courcelles during her loneliest days with Willy, of the society of women surrounding Missy, of her own ventures into both milieux, and of her thoughts and observations on sex generally. She herself considered it her best book. 'One day others will think so too.'

Those of her works which like this one are of a personal experience, admittedly autobiographical, were nearly always written at a great distance. Twenty years had passed since her relationship with Missy, and nearly thirty since those lonely days in the rue de Courcelles. And with one exception she never made notes. Her sense-memory was incredibly rich, as was her emotional one; the inaccuracy of the details of facts and dates gave precedence to a larger truth. Her memory neither distorts nor romanticises; it recollects the daily atmosphere of relationships and their surroundings with immediacy because she was so totally absorbed in whatever she was experiencing that she could not at the time stand back and take note. The moment, the incident, penetrated her and was stored in her senses' memory. 'Don't write your copy while you are away,' she advised Renée Hamon, 'it will seem unrecognisable to you when you get back. One doesn't write a love story whilst one is making love.'

And in *L'Etoile Vesper*, which she believed would be her last book: 'I shan't leave a single note behind me, not a note, not a notebook, not the least little scrawled indication.' The one exception to this life-long preference was when the Swiss publisher, Gonin, asked her to write a book on animals, and in preparation she visited the zoo at Antwerp. There she did take notes, though she did not, in fact, use them in the essays on caged animals which form the first part of *Prisons et paradis*. She wrote on eight pages of a small lined notebook. '... a packet of pythons. Badly knotted, hanging all over the place ... a head slides out from the tangles and twists and turns and spirals. "Let me go!" says the python to himself, "You're throttling me!" She identified easily with caged animals, having suffered as one herself in her thirteen years with Willy; and with animals in their natural state from her nearness to them from childhood. She had also, since her touring days, become very much involved with performing animals; and in 1930 was invited with a number of other French journalists to Berlin, by Sarassani, the great circus king. She wrote ecstatically to Marguerite Moreno: '... everything is magnificent; the weather, the circus, the wild animals, the twenty-one nelephants [sic], the new-born camel, the tiger and lion cubs, everything.' But strangely she wrote nothing for any newspaper on the subject. Sarassani had hoped that the publicity given him by the journalists would result in his being invited to France, where he was not welcome by the indigenous circus owners, very possibly because his troupe, which included five hundred animals, was of a much higher standard. In spite of his overtures to the press, he never did get to France, and only five years after their visit he was ordered by Hitler to get rid of the Jews, Yugoslavs and Negroes he employed. He preferred to leave the country and set off for South America. Tragically, the night before embarking from Antwerp the tent housing his twenty-two elephants caught fire, and most of them were burned to death.

Remembrance of Things Past

9 rue de Beaujolais, entrance to the Palais-Royal.

SHE RETURNED FROM BERLIN TO THE apartment in Paris where she had been living, apart from the summer months, for the last three years, on the mezzanine floor of 9 rue de Beaujolais. Her secretary during those years was a young woman called Claude Chauvière, who made no bones about the fact that she was writing a book about her. It was published in 1930, and gives a picture of the warmth, the health and the vitality of Colette in her daily life:

Overflowing with life and activity she glows with physical joy, hugging to her strong heart everything that quivers with life, in order to embrace it, crush it, draw the very marrow out of it ... she creates disorder around her ... her conversation is spiced with anecdotes, reminiscences, comical ideas. She judges, imitates, compares, hums, and recites: she is never melancholy, sometimes furious.... To be at ease she needs us to be comfortable; 'Are you warm Claude?' (to Pauline) 'Turn on the radiator; she's pale, she's cold. ... Maurice, put the salad into the dressing, it's better that way. ... Souci *will* you go to sleep! And quicker than that!'

That year, 1930, the book which many French people consider Colette's masterpiece was published: the third evocation of her mother, *Sido*.

La Maison de Claudine had been composed of anecdotal chapters: 'My Mother and the Curate', 'My Mother and the Animals', etc. In *La Naissance du jour* she had quoted from her mother's letters, and sketched evocatively her memory. Now in *Sido* there was a full-length portrait, though the chapter called 'Sido' is only twenty-one printed pages long: a humorous and loving insight into this extraordinary yet ordinary human being, this simple yet many-sided country woman, capable of jealousy though never of meanness, of partisanship, of censoriousness, a fighter against injustice, a small earthy creature in a bundle of red petticoats with an unlikely background of culture, knowledge of the arts, and of city life. The book contains shorter chapters on the Captain and on the two boys, *les sauvages*, and is interwoven with the child Colette seen as perceptively and as humorously as any of them. Though *Sido* is rich in

PREVIOUS PAGE 'There were never any more beautiful eyes in the world, nor any which knew better how to see.' (Maurice Goudeket *Près de Colette*)

memory, it is not embroidered. It is as short as a long short story. Colette had never obeyed any rules of length, any more than she had kept separate reality and fiction, or past and present. The impression remains with *Sido* that for Colette the past runs concurrently with the present, and that her total immersion in her present has never ousted her past.

She had seemingly also been able to dispense in her life with the rule of place; not only on the stage where she was of necessity living in two places at once, on the theatre boards and in whatever imaginary country the choreographer had set for her, but off-stage, in her own person, she felt herself to be in many places at once:

'At the slightest stir of memory, Monts-Boucons comes back to me.'
(*Mes apprentissages*)

You think she's sitting here close to us, don't you? But at the same time she's sitting on the cool rock on the other side of the valley, and on the low scented branch of the silvery pine. You think she's asleep; but at this very moment she's in the kitchen-garden, picking the white strawberry that smells of squashed ant. She's under the rose-tunnel breathing, almost tasting, the oriental scent of a thousand winy roses that have blossomed in the sun of a single day. Though she doesn't stir and her eyes are closed, she's on every lawn, in every tree and in every flower. Like a phantom as blue as the air, she leans out of every window of her vine-bearded house at the same time. Her spirit runs like a subtle blood along the veins of all the leaves, caresses the velvet of the geraniums and the varnish of the cherry and twines itself round the dust-powdered snake in the hollow of the yellow path....

That was at Monts-Boucons, Kiki-la-Doucette talking to Toby-Chien. But the ability of her spirit to inhabit other places was not confined to nature; in her old age, bedridden, writing of gangster-children, commercial-minded children, or the screaming children seen from her window overlooking the gardens of the Palais-Royal she expresses this oneness again, but differently: 'I haven't the heart to reprove them ... because I contemplate them, and in con-templating them I make them mine.... That evil child is secretly mine, as is mine the animal with whom I exchange a sign, as is mine one of the flowers down there because I am perhaps the only one who knows its name....'

In the August of that year, 1930, Colette returned as usual to La Treille muscate to find that Saint-Tropez had been invaded by the fancy-dress ball set and their retinue of *Vogue* photographers.

The harbour had become inaccessible, blocked by three rows of Hispano-Suizas and Bugattis. The little port was ruined and Colette wrote to Marguerite Moreno that Sainte-Maxime was worse: 'They don't even bathe,' she wrote in disgust. Luckily La Treille muscate was not so easily accessible and as long as she did not go to the harbour to shop, she was not lionised. After August, to her relief, Saint-Tropez returned to its natural state, the shops became once more village shops, cardboard dolls giving place to smoked herrings; fishing boats bobbed in the harbour and the view of the sea from L'Escale where Colette and her friends sometimes dined on the pavement was no longer blotted out by large and expensive cars.

Life at La Treille muscate was back to normal. 'Maurice works (sic) in the garden with astonishment, clumsiness, and a thousand questions,' she wrote to Marguerite Moreno. Goudeket in fact, though he had introduced Colette to the South of France, had been brought up not only in ignorance but in fear of the countryside; his father's theory being that trees absorb all available oxygen, not leaving enough to keep human beings alive. 'You don't look well,' he would say to Maurice's mother, 'I bet you've been to the Bois de Boulogne again.' But though Goudeket was far from understanding the earth, he understood Colette's understanding, and would watch her whilst she gardened with vigour, or sat scratching up the earth with her fingers, excitedly smelling, as were her cat and dog, the secrets that lay below the surface.

Later in 1930 a film version by Solange Bussy was made of *La Vagabonde*, and Colette's daughter, now seventeen, was employed as an assistant director. Film life suited her talents admirably, whereas her mother had always been, and remained, a little in awe of it; she admired the extraordinary dedication of those who earn their living by it, but never felt at ease in its atmosphere.

Colette de Jouvenel at seventeen.

I still ask myself [Colette wrote of another film, *La Divine*, which she watched being made] from where do they draw their energy ... those interminable workdays which begin at dawn under false lights, ignore meal-times, disregard the limits of human endurance, and sometimes finish – those also acting in the theatre have to be there by eight o'clock – only to recommence sometime after midnight. For people of my generation the cinema will always have a defensive aura, uneasily penetrated. My daughter shares the lot, the impassibility of the actors and the other film workers, like them she rests standing up, and like them keeps quiet for long periods.

One day in the coldest week of February, I was at the Billancourt studios where fifty half-nude young women were filming some music-hall scenes. For seven consecutive hours they submitted to the extreme temperatures of a canvas-covered yard, made icy by the east wind, then briefly overheated under a catastrophe of lights. At the brief commands of Max Ophüls, they went up and down the rough wood steps without hand-rails, and ran, performed evolutions, with inexhaustible grace. No-one, in spite of empty stomachs, allowed himself to faint. At an order from Ophüls, 'Your feet can be heard on the steps! Take off your slippers!' fifty young women, including Simone Berriau took off their shoes without a word and ran, barefoot, on the unplaned wood, among the rubber snakes, iron filings, bits of crumbling plaster and nails.

It was that same day that a snake-tamer's hands laid on Simone Berriau's shoulders a living python nearly as heavy as a man. 'What will he do?' I had asked him a short while before; he raised his shoulders, uncertain: 'One doesn't know ... he's young, you see, and intelligent. ... He's not vicious, mind you, but he doesn't know the lady ... it's best to let him alone. At the worst I always carry. ...' He showed me with simplicity a double-edged sword. Then he took three yards of python from a suit-case, which was being kept warm on a radiator. When he placed the formidable actor on the shoulders of the 'Divine', dressed as a Hindu dancing girl, she stumbled for a moment, then stood up straight; then she was left alone with 'Joseph' and both were subjected to the pitiless glare of the lights. At first she had the serpent at hip level. He encircled her firmly and deployed his agile head towards her neck and throat. He prospected her breasts, which he tasted with his long double-pronged tongue. A kind of anguished smile swam across the dancing-girl's face, mouth half-open on shining teeth; the serpent's head disappeared behind a shoulder, dragged the body in ineffable serpentine progression, and I thought the ordeal was at an end. ... But at the summit of the gold and silver coiffure the python's head reappeared, erect as a steel lance. Another moment and the head slid down the temple, stopped at the corner of the eyebrow, licked the cheek. ... Then Simone Berriau let fall her huge eyelids, veiling her pupils and Ophüls allowed her to be delivered. ... She shook off the evil spell and asked 'How was that? Were we alright Joseph and I?'

Though Colette never became at ease in a film atmosphere, in the theatre, whether as a performer or critic, she was on ground she totally understood. Her theatre pieces for *La Revue de Paris*, and subsequently for *Le Journal*, were later gathered together in four volumes titled *La Jumelle noire*. Having performed in the theatre made her a rare critic in that she could distinguish the work of the actor from that of the director or the playwright, so she knew on whose shoulders to place her praise or blame.

On a revival of *La Dame aux camélias*, she wrote:

This useless piece belongs henceforth (common sense demands it) in a drawer, on which some eccentric has described the contents as 'bits of string ... useless'. How can one explain the infatuation of certain actresses, and not inconsiderable ones, with such a play?... Today, Robert Gaillard bores himself profoundly as Armand Duval, a role which resembles a deserted corridor. The principal role has tempted the energies of an actress-singer, who tones down her gestures, her voice, her walk, even her magnificent hair to its requirements, and who would do better to lend them to the freedoms – even the crudities – of some realistic and modern role. I know one can offer such counsel to Madame Claudia Victrix. It is not success which attracts her, but the attempt, the work, even the most fearless daring.

Nor is she afraid of uninhibited praise. On Mistinguett: 'She has returned. Once more she participates in our social life. Once more in the centre of Paris there is a luminous point that she warms each night with her presence. Paris only wishes for one thing. The eternity of Mistinguett.'

She is exceptionally perceptive about Shakespeare, and the French attitude towards his plays. From her notice of *Richard III*: '... it is not to them but to their director that I address one single (but important) reproach: the actors throw a gloom over the text, take the tragic too seriously. Am I wrong? If one reads the play, everyone, even the murdered, seem gayer.'

And on a production of *Coriolanus*: '... an excellent Shakespeare made lukewarm in the French manner. What is lacking in the French *Coriolanus* is warmth and humour, caprice and peculiarity.'

Though essentially French her instinct recognised the English flavour as few other French people, including translators, have done.

In 1931 the forgotten Willy died. He had outlived by too many years his popularity in a period of punsters and pasticheurs. Not long after the 1914–18 war he had been asked by one of his friends to write a piece for a magazine, but he himself knew that he was out of touch. The world in which he had shone was gone; that world in which through pure malice he could ensure that a musician he had a personal antipathy to, Erik Satie, would not be taken seriously during his lifetime. He retained a scant number of friends, but he had no place in a society which through pain and terror and disillusionment had learned a new set of values. Not long before he died he admitted that his part in the *Claudines* had been only 'that of a marvelling professor who insisted on seeing his pupil's work'. It was not however until 1948, seventeen years after his death, that Flammarion, in publishing the collected works of Colette, put her name alone on the *Claudine* books. This decision was again reversed the year after Colette's death, when Willy's son, Jacques Gauthier-Villars, insisted that the *Claudines* should subsequently be printed as by WILLY and COLETTE.

Colette did not write of those days with Willy until five years after his death when she managed, in *Mes apprentissages*, the incredible feat of what seems like total recall of thoughts, sensations and emotions after forty years. And she achieves it in the most extraordinary way. She seems at the beginning of the book not to know where it will lead her. A series of essays begins: on a child, on La Belle Otéro, the Spanish dancer, on a woman who tells of a jealous affair, and then, quite inconsequentially comes the sentence 'but there is one person I shall never understand' ... and there is the key, with which she unlocks the memory of her young heart, her shock, her disillusionment, her illness and her dismissal, wounds seemingly never quite scarred over.

Of course Willy's remaining friends threw angry accusations at her, but she had refrained until now – or perhaps not wished to write during his lifetime – from setting down the unlikely tale she so convincingly tells. The scandal of Willy's treatment of her over a period of thirteen years is alarming, and yet to Willy's Parisian contemporaries this was far more acceptable than the sight of two women kissing on stage at the Moulin Rouge. Morality perhaps will always be a subject for contention.

Mes apprentissages was not written until 1936. Between Willy's death and its publication Colette was at her most prolific. She wrote in those five years not only *Prisons et paradis* and *Ces Plaisirs* ... but two novels and (her energy at sixty being inexhaustible) she started on a totally new career, as a beautician. All this in spite of falling and fracturing her hip, an accident which probably caused the arthritis which some years later was to immobilise her.

It happened at Saint-Tropez and with her usual dislike of pain and ill-health she treated the accident with forceful humour.

Souci could not bear to see me cry [she wrote in *Journal à rebours*]. Nor most certainly could I break a leg without putting her life in jeopardy: her heart couldn't stand it. After the first moments – one is not in too much agony to begin with from a broken leg – I was able to call anxiously from my stretcher 'Look after the bitch ... take care ...' because Souci unable to speak or moan, was behaving as she did in a nightmare, craving air, and hanging out a chalky purple tongue: 'Give her some cold water. Squeeze a lemon into her mouth, don't you see she's about to faint?' But they poured eau de cologne on my forehead, I who was in no danger. . . .

That was written years later, but even a few days after the accident she could write to her daughter: 'There is always a comic side to these great cataclysms. Maurice who was turning the car round to drive back heard me cry out, saw me rolling about, and in his panic drove the car into a ditch! Dear Moune stayed to look after me and forgot to go back to her house for lunch, so Luc came to look for her. Hearing about the accident, he then drives the Fiat into the ditch! Any more and there wouldn't have been enough ditches for all our friends' cars.'

One of the novels of this period was the famous *La Chatte*. It embodies three of her previous themes: the search for the return to an earthly paradise; the link between human beings and animals; and the ravages of jealousy. Like Chéri, Alain seeks to recapture his youth through his first love, who is not an old cocotte this time, but a Cat.

'. . . under the blue lantern, which is in reality nothing more than a commercial lamp at the end of a long extensible X; and covered with a blue paper skirt.' (*Le Fanal bleu*)

Most of the critics dismissed the story indignantly as 'a fine talent demeaned by a ludicrous theme'. But Edmond Jaloux called it 'a masterpiece of art, of classic perfection, told with the maximum of truth, of intelligence and of poetry'. Colette is not afraid of heightened drama, though the means by which she arouses one's senses to the point of participating in the action is as economical as it is breathtaking. The scene in which the young wife frenziedly jealous of the Cat throws her out of the seventh-floor window is as vertiginous as Colette's earlier news report of going up in a balloon. 'She [Camille] had the time to hear the claws scratching on the plaster of the wall, to see the blue body of Saha twisted into an "S" clutching the air with the leaping power of the trout; then she retreated and leaned against the wall.' This is not the end of the book. The Cat's fall is broken and it lives. Now Alain and Camille have to face each other.

Colette does not blame the murderous little wife: for all her own aching longing to recapture the happiness of childhood, she states quite clearly in the last sentence of the book that the life of the present is the destiny of the human race, and for a human being to seek to return to his primitive state is abnormal and regressive.

When Alain throws the word 'monster' at Camille for what she has done, she throws it back at him, and as she leaves, 'Alain, half supine, was playing with the first green prickly chestnuts of August in an agile palm that was hollowed like a paw.'

The classic economy of style, the unveiling of a world of meaning in a sentence, are at the heart of her writing, as many eminent French writers have always recognised.

Her recurring themes of love and jealousy and the lucidity of her writing ensure her a vast public. Her imagery is immediate, sprinkled with those fish, fruit or flowers that possibly few of her readers may have looked at with much attention, but can nevertheless recognise and respond to at once; the similes always referring backwards to a more primitive manifestation of life: the nails of the new-born child resembling the convex scale of the pink shrimp, the kiss that is a palpitation of two coupled pistils, the falling cat clutching the air with the leaping power of the trout. . . .

Aside from the immediacy of the imagery, she has the biologist's care for exactitude; there is no romanticism. The images do not bend to meet the human need, they remain firmly in their own world, yet enable the reader to hold the moment, to fix the image more precisely. But in spite of her lucidity, and in spite of the reader's immediate response to her evocation, she remains appallingly difficult to translate. Raymond Mortimer in his preface to Roger Senhouse's translation of *Chéri* writes: 'Her vocabulary is

'I shall be happy to welcome you, Madame, at 6 rue de Miromesnil on Wednesday, June 1st.' (Invitation to the opening of Colette's salon)

enormous, and savoury with archaic and regional words. From her imagination images rush profusely forth.... She can foreshorten the French language as boldly as Mallarmé, she has it trained to obey her caprices like a pony in a circus. All of which is a perpetual feast to the reader, a chronic headache to the translator....'

The ingredients of *La Chatte*, apart from its literary beauty, are a mixture of imagination, portraiture, and a small amount of fact. The portrait is that of the cat Saha who is the centre of the drama; a portrait of Colette's own cat, La Chatte, the One and Only, the Chartreuse she had bought at five months old and who lived, the best-beloved of both Colette and Maurice Goudeket, until 1939. Alain and Camille are only lightly based on a young married couple she knew in Saint-Tropez, and whom she wrote of in her essay, 'Nudité'. The seventh-floor apartment the characters live in was one she knew in Neuilly, and is as essential to her story as the other ingredients.

The shorter novel of this rich period, *Duo*, may seem to have the same theme as both *Chéri* and *La Chatte*, that of a despairing yearning to return; but as Margaret Davies perceptively points out in her assessment of Colette as a writer, *Duo* is a musical composition, and 'a duet between tenor and soprano: from their initial satisfied love-song to the idyllic accompaniment of the nightingales, through the harsh, frenetic discords of the man's discovery, the gradual disintegration of his voice into staccato sobs and silences, his obsessive rhythmical pacing that matches his rhythmical obsession, his reiterated nagging, the identification of the woman's voice with comforting, household noises, to the climax of the obscene jingles in the discovered letter ringing round and round in the man's head, and finally the utter silence of his resignation as he walks out silently in the muted dawn into the silent element of water, and is covered by its little waves beating an almost imperceptible rhythm.'

In *Duo* the language of words and music had become interwoven just as the past and present had become one in *La Naissance du jour*.

With these two achievements she reached the pinnacle of expression of her deepest roots, but at sixty-one she had still twenty years of creativity left in her, as well as the vigour to start on a new career, researching and promoting her own beauty products; 'I have one perfume just right,' she wrote to Marguerite Moreno, 'another nearly; a water – that is to say a liquid – for the skin which is a marvel, another from the white of egg, for different skins.' She recalled her mother's homely country recipes, based her products on the herbs and essences she knew well and loved. After conferences and demonstrations all over France she opened her salon in Paris at no. 6 rue de Miromesnil on 1 June 1932.

André Maginot (later, famous as the creator of the Maginot Line) had suggested the career to her some years before. She was persuaded that it was a good idea and set about it with great enthusiasm. Goudcket was not so convinced; he realised the enormous amount of work it would demand, as Colette was of course determined to do all the work and the promotion herself, even to making-up customers with her own hands. But Goudeket was not one to interfere with Colette's independence.

The project in any case only lasted a year. It proved financially unsuccessful, and Colette was always being sidetracked by her customers into signing and discussing her books. After a year of extremely hard work, she realised that she must abandon it.

She was living at this time in an apartment on the sixth floor of the Hôtel Claridge. She still wrote to and received visits from her two stepsons; sometimes she would even write and ask Renaud for news of the young Colette, who was absorbed in her film work, addressing him as she had always done as 'Dear Kid' or sometimes 'Dear old Kid', or 'Dear One-time Kid', and ending with 'I am still your old friend'. On one occasion when he went to visit her in the hotel, he got into the lift with a short fat man, smartly dressed with hat and shoes to match his suit – 'I thought he was some gay old dog, and I found he was visiting the same apartment as I was. Colette introduced me: "You know the Marquise de Belbeuf?"'

Until 1935 it had not occurred to Goudeket and Colette to get married, but it suddenly struck them that they were making difficulties for themselves and also incurring unnecessary expense in order to seem to be keeping up the proprieties. They married unceremoniously in April, and in the June were grateful for the decision they had made, as they were invited to make a two-day visit to New York on the maiden voyage of the *Normandie*. 'If we had not been married,' Goudeket writes, 'our living together in prim New York would have presented not inconsiderable problems for us.'

On this rushed visit they did nothing more, he reports, than behave like a honeymoon couple from Detroit or Pittsburgh. They went to the top of the Empire State Building, to Central Park and Harlem, they spent hours in Woolworths which bored him but delighted her, and they saw Mae West in a movie at the Roxy. On the way back from the cinema he said to her: '"Conjure up a cat for us", and there, conjured up or not was the cat with its tail in the air, running towards Colette as if it had found a relation, and mewing. "At last someone who speaks French," she cried. She sat down, as was right and proper, on the edge of the pavement and the conversation began.'

'We visited the top of the Empire State Building, where of course we had ourselves photographed. . . .' (Maurice Goudeket *Près de Colette*)

That same year, and within a few months of her mother, Colette de Jouvenel also married – a large and bearded Dr Dausse. Like her grandmother Sido and like her mother, her first choice upset and disappointed her. She came, shamefaced, very few weeks after her wedding to tell her mother of what she imagined was her disgrace. But Colette behaved with her accustomed brusquerie towards social conventions: 'Don't stand there suffering and stammering,' she said, 'I understand. You've not got the right one, and there's no use making yourself miserable any longer. You're much too young to be unhappy. Now you'd better go and tell your father about it.' Henry de Jouvenel reacted as individually as Colette had done; and did not question her obvious and immature excuse: 'Oh, if you're bored,' he said, 'that's the worst possible thing. You can't be expected to put up with boredom.' 'So you see,' said Colette de Jouvenel, 'my parents had great understanding. They didn't waste time thinking what the divorce would mean socially or in any other way: they thought of what was best for me.'

But both parents were absorbed in their own lives, and Colette asked Renaud if he would care for his twenty-two-year-old step-sister for a few weeks whilst the girl recovered from her difficulties. Renaud undertook to look after her, but with bad grace; he confessed to not liking his sister, nor her friends; and to finding his step-mother lacking in feeling under the circumstances. 'You'd think by her letters and her writings that she loved her daughter,' he said, 'but she was really inhuman.' He also (erroneously) believed that his sister could not go to her father because she never visited him; that she saw him as irritable, bad-tempered, and (using the same word as he had for Colette) 'inhuman'.

A very few months later, in the October of 1935, Henry de Jouvenel died quite suddenly, aged fifty-nine. Since his divorce from Colette he had continued to be a successful politician: Minister of Education in Poincaré's government in 1924, Minister of Overseas France under Daladier, High Commissioner in Syria in 1925, and in 1932 French Ambassador to Italy. The background to the novel she wrote six years after his death, *Julie de Carneilhan*, may have reflected their life together, but she states specifically that Espivant is not a portrait of Henry de Jouvenel. Anatole de Monzie wrote to her on 1 June 1942. 'I found nothing in this novel which evoked the *personnage* of de Jouvenel. I am amazed when *they* speak to me about it. *They* with their knowing air pretend to identify Henry de Jouvenel with the character in your book.' Colette replied: 'If you didn't recognise him in Espivant, it's because he isn't there, and my little character is imaginary, and never aimed to be anything more – or less. No, Espivant is not de Jouvenel.'

When she portrayed people and events she had known, she wrote frankly, giving names to the people and the places. Willy is Willy in *Mes apprentissages*, Sido is *Sido*. With her novels she did what every novelist does, basing her people and places on her own experiences, and mixing the ingredients with her imagination in a variety of ways, so that, as in *La Chatte* one sentence from a young man acquaintance about his offended taste in seeing his new young wife walk about in the nude every morning, gave her the clue to an imagined relationship which she developed in the book, adding the ingredient of someone she knew intimately, her own Chartreuse cat.

Julie de Carneilhan was written six years after de Jouvenel's death. In the meantime, in 1936, honours accumulated; and these entailed making speeches, which she did not enjoy doing. Speaking on the stage, disguised as someone else in front of a darkened auditorium or even lecturing about animals to strangers was nothing like as frightening as making a reception speech to a group of well-known people. She could not hide behind identification with another, nor behind the protection of a barrier of light. She was left with her rolling Rs to face her *compères*. In the February she was elected Commandeur of the Légion d'honneur. She had been elected a Chevalier as early as 1920, and an Officier in 1928. She was to become Grand Officier the year before her death, in 1953.

In the April of 1936 she was offered the chair vacated by the death of the poetess Anna de Noailles, in the Belgian Royal Academy of French Language and Literature; and had to prepare a long speech about her predecessor. The Comtesse and Colette had corresponded since 1904, always with mutual eulogies, and always on ceremonious terms. It would have been difficult for Colette to have responded with her usual colloquial earthiness to the famous poetess's very sincere condescension.

Cocteau, in *Portraits-souvenir* gives this description of the Comtesse:

At table she wanted all the guests to listen to her and remain silent. . . . If she drank she would hold her glass in her right hand and make a sign with her left that she must not be interrupted. And the guests obeyed. Let us admit, she sometimes cheated . . . some did not notice, some laughed up their sleeves, and others suffered. I was among the latter. I pitied her, I saw her getting into difficulties, being muddled and taking short cuts. Anything rather than return to silence! . . . For this intuitive woman imagined that she had the culture of a Goethe. The astonishing electricity that escaped from her, the lightning which played about her, the waves which emanated from her, she persisted in taking all this for intelligence.

In unofficial honours lists Colette had always been one or two votes behind Anna de Noailles. Magazines held their own referendums; in 1921 the readers of *Les Tablettes*, electing a 'Queen of Letters' gave Anna de Noailles 765 votes and Colette 764. In 1923 *Eve* chose Anna de Noailles with 2,397 votes and Colette followed with 2,363. In 1934 *Minerva* voted Anna de Noailles Princess of Poetry, Colette Princess of Prose, Cécile Sorel Princess of the Theatre and Marie Curie Princess of Science.

In her speech at the Belgian Academy, Colette carefully avoided talking about her predecessor's poetry as she had avoided writing about the politics of politicians for newspapers: and confined herself instead and as usual to a description of her subject:

... I saw Madame de Noailles focus her eyes above the head of the person speaking to her, towards a field of invisible happenings. A few photographs have happily caught the dreamy gentleness of her look at such moments. But no portrait could translate for us the return of Madame de Noailles to reality, to the insipid and displeasing person at her side. She had a sudden and annihilating way of re-focussing her enraptured gaze and planting it on the offender with a look of terrible humour, of crushing astonishment, of questioning surprise, that could only be translated by the words 'Why aren't you dead?'

'... grandiloquent, voluble ... tossing out innumerable utterances ... Madame de Noailles nevertheless gave very little of herself.' (Colette's speech at the Belgian Academy)

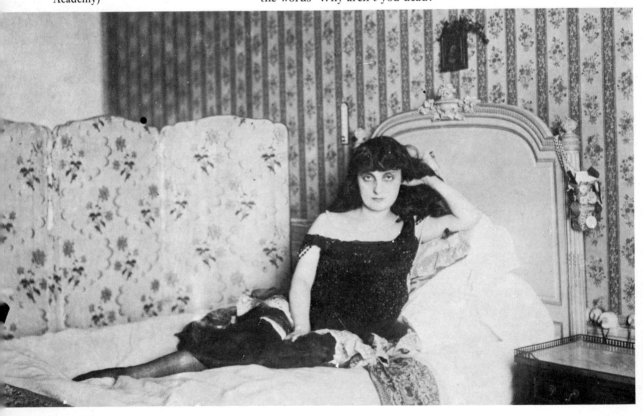

'... racked with fear and anxiety, she was longing for the end of the world. Yet when she stood up, very straight in a simple black frock ... her voice was firm, and the hands that held the sheets of her discourse did not tremble at all....' (Maurice Goudeket *Près de Colette*)

In 1938 Colette moved into an apartment on the first floor of 9 rue de Beaujolais. She had lived in the same building some ten years before, but this time her apartment overlooked the gardens of the Palais-Royal, and here she remained until her death. She had changed flats in Paris and houses in different parts of France eighteen times or more, each time with the contradictory feelings of the nomad who must continually renew herself, and the bourgeoise who must make a permanent nest. She was still in other respects 'on the move' – she was sent to Fez the following year to write some articles for *Paris-Soir* – but an arthritic hip was soon to immobilise her. Renée Hamon – 'le Petit Corsaire' as Colette called her, and which she used for the title of her travel book – wrote in her diary after visiting Colette in her new apartment: 'At sixty-five she is still a hot-blooded animal, vibrant, incapable of accepting the slightest hindrance....'

Colette had visited North Africa a number of times for work or for pleasure before her commission from *Paris-Soir* just before the war, once at the invitation of El Glaoui and in 1931 on a conference tour, and her impressions are vividly recorded in the second half of *Prisons et paradis.* In writing of places or people she only knew as a stranger she never attempted to penetrate further than the surface of what a visitor could know or sense. But her writings open corridors of possibilities in the reader's mind. To Colette, what was only skin-deep, was not at all a camouflage, but a clue to what lay below. Beauty was to her the truthful outward show of an inner life, the tip of the iceberg which nevertheless predicted the same nature below. She would always be a prey to physical beauty. She was ravished by a butterfly, by her own child's six-year-old limbs, by the bulldog Souci's eyes which revealed the unquiet little soul that swam through them.

A physical description of a small child in Africa, seen very much with an outsider's eyes, nevertheless opens the imagination onto a different continent:

She was as much as five years old, and resplendent with melancholy coquetry. She had overlarge eyebrows painted across her forehead, a proud, plump-lipped mouth, strong teeth and ageless langorous eyes between eyelashes thickened with make-up. A blue star marked each rounded cheekbone, a blue arrow divided her chin. Groups of blue signs joined her eyebrows between the eyes. Beneath the reddish shapeless rag on her head, two miniscule and dusty plaits curled round her ears like rams' horns. Elsewhere the remnants of cotton strips revealed here a slender knee, there an insubstantial thigh. The stony slope on which she sat imitated exactly the colour of her skin, a light yellow mysteriously blended with pink, and the motionless little girl seemed born but an instant before ... modelled out of a handful of desert.

As the war approached a number of her own generation of friends died. Polaire wrote to her from hospital: 'They give me frightful injections in the lung. My little dog, who comes to see me twice a week, despises me because I'm ill. ... It upsets me very much.' The once famous little eighteen-inch waisted girl, who had recently been billed in America as 'the Ugliest Woman in the World', died in 1939. Léo, Colette's brother, died just before the declaration of war, Missy was to die by her own hand,* alone and poverty-stricken; though the kindly and generous Sacha Guitry provided her with food till the end. Guitry himself died during the war, and on 26 March 1939, Colette wrote to the critic Edmond Jaloux '... our beloved Cat died five weeks ago. And one month before, on Sunday 17 March, the bulldog died. Especially because of the Cat, Maurice and I are totally downcast.'

So deeply was she affected by the death of the cat and dog that for the rest of her life – though friends and sometimes strangers brought their pets to visit her – she lived without an animal of her own.

When, a few years later, she was confined to her room, she devoted that thought and care, previously given to her animals, to something else which also moved, ate, changed, and needed her attention: 'Now I possess only one living creature, which is the fire. It is at the same time my guest and my work. I know how to protect the fire, to succour the fire. ... I know that it doesn't like even numbers, that three logs burn better than two and seven than four, and that, like any other beast, it likes its belly rubbed from underneath.' Even the primordial was thought of and treated on the same level as plant, animal and man.

* 'A sort of Hara-Kiri' Colette wrote to Marquente Moreno.

The Occupation

OPPOSITE German supply column passes through the Avenue Foch.

THE DECLARATION OF WAR ON 3 September 1939 surprised Colette and Goudeket whilst they were staying with Léopold Marchand in Dieppe.

They returned at once to Paris, and for the next eight months broadcast to America on Radio Paris-Mondial nightly in the blacked-out city.

... since it is now obligatory to carry a gas-mask, and within a week the women have turned this cylindrical case into an object of personal taste. Tartan-covered, dressed in leather like a travelling case, clothed in silk, striped like a little umbrella, or else in assorted materials and colours to match a costume; worn at the waist, thrown over the shoulder, carried on the back, haversack-mask, pocket-mask, handbag-mask. ... I wouldn't swear that all the cases held the regulation contents, judging by my own in which I carry so conveniently from Les Halles one of the last of the little melons, a pound of grapes, some nuts ... let's not go into it too deeply. The Parisian, rebellious by nature, will always prefer convenience to security. . . .

But in the June of 1940 came the occupation of Paris by the Germans, and the great exodus began.

Colette and Goudeket joined the long long slow queue of vehicles heading for the unoccupied zone. They went to Curemonte in Corrèze where Colette de Jouvenel was living. '... two medieval castles, lofty and narrow, barely ten yards apart ... threatened not with ruin, as this had already occurred, but with complete collapse.... But the outhouses, running the length of the enclosing wall ... made a comfortable dwelling.'

But once arrived Colette pined to return to Paris: 'These three weeks without communication have been unbearably hard,' she wrote to Germaine Beaumont, 'no petrol, no post, no telegram, no telephone, no butter, no passers-by ... the privation of all news.'

'I'm used to spending my wars in Paris,' she said, and Goudeket suggested that they went to their newspaper offices in Lyons and prepare their return journey from there. But to get petrol was not

PREVIOUS PAGE '... don't you know that the German armies are in Paris?' (L'Etoile Vesper)

easy even with the help of Edouard Herriot who was a great friend and admirer of Colette. They eventually started on their journey, only to be stopped by a German at the control post of the occupied zone. He passed Goudeket, but suspected Colette: 'You, Jewess', and to Pauline: 'You, *certainly* Jewess.'

'I don't really know what possessed me,' wrote Goudeket, '... what stupid pride, what insane revolt against a ban which I thought odious: "You're utterly mistaken," I said to the German in his own tongue, "I alone here am of Jewish birth."'

As a result of course they had to return to Lyons, and three weeks later made the attempt again, this time armed with a letter from the Swedish Consulate, which worked wonders. Once back in the Palais-Royal, Colette could do little more than watch the microcosm of Paris from her window overlooking the Palais gardens, 'humbly among those who do nothing but wait'.

What 'resistance', what war can I speak of, other than those I have witnessed? ... From the corner of this window I saw Paris sink into suffering, darken with grief and humiliation, but also, each day, increasingly resist. ... During the Occupation this Palais-Royal was a stronghold of pinched adventurous old men, of disrespectful children, of shopkeepers without goods, of derisive adolescent girls, pure Parisian types. ...

But she was not only waiting, with tenacity and loathing; she was also writing. The background to the book is of course Paris. Paris of the Twenties. The Paris of Espivant, because this is the year in which she wrote *Julie de Carneilhan*. It is the story of a woman separated from her husband, and is composed of the subtle boxes of tricks within tricks that are the 'games' people play. Each time the trick is revealed it shows, paradoxically, that it is not that trick but another that is being played. Julie and the reader are tricked together, and make the discovery of the trickery together. It is also the last of the books on the theme of a return to Paradise. As in most of the novels, the moment of return is only reached at the end of the book, sometimes, as in *La Chatte*, in the very last sentence. But the emotion of return (one cannot call it a philosophy because in each case it is a conclusion that has nothing cerebral about it) is totally different each time, just as the stories that precede it vary greatly in their milieux and in their characters. Claudine was refreshed by her return and made strong enough to cope with her present difficulties. Alain's return was regressive, unhealthy: he himself was happy with what he found, but one is left with a distaste in the mouth. Chéri's return was a shock to him – the past had changed, unrecognisably, and there was nothing left for him but suicide. Colette herself both inside and outside her books recaptures it, re-tastes it, but does not let it deny the present. Julie de Carneilhan, preparing to leave Paris with her brother one early misty morning to return to the countryside of her childhood, realises that *he* is taking with him his beloved horse, whilst she will be leaving behind the thing she loves best in the world. Colette had only very recently left the Germans occupying Paris and gone to a peaceful countryside, only to realise after she got there that she had not taken her beloved Paris with her.

It is as if Colette questioned herself anew every time she wrote about return, but although, with hindsight, each separate conclusion would seem to be the only one for the character she writes about, like inevitability itself, it is doubtful whether she, any more than the reader, any more than her character, was prepared when she started each book for what the outcome would be. Few writers, those of Colette's intuition least of all, know what the end of their book will be, either in a narrative or a philosophical sense. One thing springs like life itself from its predecessor, and cannot be foreseen before its proper turn to appear. A planned outcome will very often have to be scrapped, because inevitability will take its place.

So she wrote, and waited: 'to wait in Paris is to drink water from the source itself, however bitter.' But in December 1941 the waiting and the writing were replaced by personal nightmare.

In the early hours of 12 December 1941 came the ring of the bell; and Maurice Goudeket was taken from his bed and marched off to the internment camp at Compiègne, preparatory to being transported to Germany.

'Once they had gone, he and the 1,200 others of that batch, they immediately became like the nameless dead. Not a word, not a sign to tell us they were still alive.'

Although she had tapped him lightly on the shoulder and smiled a goodbye, she could never as long as she lived hear the ring of the bell without reliving the searing and fearful memory. At seventy-three she wrote 'I may not always be able to exclude from my painful memories and intermittent felicities the posthumous and frenetic life of the snake cut in two, the wriggling of the headless beetle. But it's quite enough to enlighten me as to what it is that undoes me as if I were a young woman, it's quite enough – the ring at the door, the start of the shoulder, the quiver of an eyelid.'

And in the same book, *L'Etoile Vesper*: 'Love, bread and butter of my pen and of my life! Whenever I sit down to speak ill of you, to disown or deny you, someone rings and the shock causes me to blink with the corner of an eye, to twitch a shoulder, a memory of the day when what I gained from you was taken away, that something that comforts me till the end of my life. . . . I offer you my apologies, Love, victorious opponent. . . .'

Because it was Christmas and because the French Railways said they had not enough trains to transport all the soldiers going back to Germany on leave as well as the loads of Jews, Goudeket and his batch were left behind for the time being. Colette from her window heard 'the cries and appeals of a night when the enemy took away the Jewish children of the district, separated the husbands from the wives, caged the men in one truck, the women in another, the children in a third. Can I compare my nightmare of absence with separations such as these?'

She concentrated all her efforts on trying to free him. She saw collaborators and Germans; there was no humiliation, Goudeket writes, which she would not face. Except one. A collaborator explained to her that he had got from the Germans permanent employment for Maurice in the camp, and special treatment, if in return Maurice would inform on his companions. 'I refuse,' said Colette calmly.

'I don't think you quite understand. The alternative is death. Death, do you understand, death.'

'Very well then, I choose death.'

'Not without consulting your husband, I imagine?'

'*We* choose death,' amended Colette.

On 13 February 1942 she wrote to Marguerite Moreno: 'If I haven't written to you it's because I carried for eight weeks something too heavy, my Marguerite. Maurice 'absent' since 12 December has just been given back to me.'

Though freed, he was nevertheless still hunted. To relieve her anxiety he spent a short time in the Midi, until the German occupation spread over the whole country. He came back to the Palais-Royal but was still obliged to hide.

And now in 1943 when other and younger authors were writing under the influence of the black events around them, Colette at seventy wrote the story that Europe did not know it was thirsting for – the story of incorruptible youth, a love story which ended not with her stories' usual disillusionment but with the reward of happiness; its heroine the delicious, uninhibited, honest and trusting girl, the extension of Claudine, the girl everyone had been waiting for and despaired of finding – Gigi.

In occupied Paris, in dolorous arthritic pain, her beloved Maurice in hiding, this old woman reaffirmed her, and millions of others' belief in youth and hope and incorruptibility. It is a slight, light short novel, based on the true story of a young girl, Yola Henriques, whom Colette had met as long ago as 1926, who had fallen in love with a man of fifty, that same Letellier, editor of *Le Journal* who had once refused to duel with Henry de Jouvenel. Colette set the story in

A French cattle-truck of women and children unloads at Auschwitz.

'I can hardly any longer leave this window corner in the heart, the very heart, of Paris.' (*L'Etoile Vesper*)

Paris of the 1890s, La Belle Epoque, the Paris of cocottes, of forgotten modes and manners; but its timeless belief in the regeneration of life through the young was avidly grasped first by France, then Europe, and later by America. It originally appeared in Lyons in the magazine *Présent*, and was published in book form in Lausanne in 1944 and in Paris at the end of the war. (It was later filmed in France in 1949 and adapted for Broadway by Anita Loos in 1951. Colette herself, from her wheelchair saw an unknown Audrey Hepburn playing a walk-on part in a film being made in Monte Carlo. 'There', she said, in the hotel foyer, 'there is our Gigi for America.')

But in 1943 when she was writing it, Paris was still German-occupied, no end of the war was in sight: 'Like the other districts of Paris, the Palais-Royal had its maquis. It held its hidden parachutists, its Englishmen sheltered in risk and silence, its protected Jews, its children rescued from a stern fate, its defaulters. . . .' And Maurice Goudeket, though 'freed' from Compiègne, was still obliged to hide to avoid recapture when the hunts were on from early evening till early morning. 'He would make his way in the evening from attic to attic, in our district, or in the Etoile.'

Then in July 1944 came that strange whiff of hope.

We were still in the troubled times of contradictory rumours, clandestine radios, whispered denials. . . . Then voices, our own, were raised, shouting aloud the names they had only whispered the day before: Leclerc, Koenig. . . . In the final hours the great captains lost their names, were called gloriously

'THEY have reached Anthony. . . . THEY have taken the heights at Châtillon. . . . No, THEY are still fighting. . . . THEY are repairing the road to let the tanks through. . . . THEY are nearly here. . . . THEY are here! . . .'

Colette was seventy-two at the end of the war. There are moments in her future works in which she recalls those years, but once the nightmare was over, it did not expunge what still concerned her most: the life around her; memories of childhood; recollections of music-hall; friends; places, plants; and work itself. She had taken up tapestry not having seriously considered that writing would any longer be a daily necessity. But in *Belles Saisons*, written in 1945, she finds that it is.

And here it comes, from the far distance, an obsession half-a-century old, a tired serpent, a suggestion which my hand, now that it holds a needle in place of a pen, has ceased to be wary of; here it comes . . . the elements of a phrase . . . worse than the phrase itself (though less exacting because it comes from oneself) the idea. . . . An idea, very far away, stirs, seeks an outlet, calls half-asleep for the aid of words.

She could not relinquish words, but she had become increasingly immobilised and in pain. 'The worst, for an arthritic like myself, is certainly not travel, if it's by car. The worst is ten paces across the room, five yards along the garden path, it is nights broken by un-adulterated, sudden and biting pains, and the thoughtless, youthful, lively movement which aspires to pick up the walking-stick, reach for the book, – O arrant youth, agility become purely mental, and punished as soon as it pulls on its leash; stairs, descended in humilia-tion and with guile: shall I never stop when meeting a stranger, pretending, as I stand still that I'm putting on a glove, rummaging in my bag?'

She went for a cure to Uriage, and to see doctors in Monte Carlo and Geneva, but sometimes the cures – and they did not cure her – were as painful as the arthritis, and she eventually decided to remain in her divan-bed, her 'raft' as she called it, which was

The relief of Paris. 'Happy were those who wept, laughed, cheered ... embraced strangers....' (*L'Etoile Vesper*)

pushed up against the window overlooking the gardens of the Palais-Royal, in the 'red room' with its red wallpaper and red furniture coverings, surrounded by her collections of butterflies and paperweights. She would take no sedative: 'Aspirin', she said to Maurice Goudeket, 'changes the colour of my thoughts. It makes me gloomy.' And on another occasion, 'I want to know just how far I can go.'

Friends, acquaintances, neighbours, children, and animals visited her.

'It was in 1950 that we went to Monte Carlo for the first time.' (Maurice Goudeket *Près de Colette*)

Come in, it's the appointed time, you whom I call my idleness and my recreation. Come in, you who scratch at my door to spare me the shock, the alarm of the bell ... come in with your rubber boots or your fine tailor-made, you with your woollen scarf round a muzzle frozen by the wind, from your bicycle.... Come in you who have suffered melting snow and wintry blast to hear a fine concert. Come in, you who run in search every day for what you and yours need. Put down your inseparable basket, let's extol the clandestine piece of hake, veal chop, or coffee.... Come in my neighbour the poet, my neighbour the playwright, my neighbour the painter, come in pairs my charming frock-coated doctors, exclaim how well I look. Come in, yet another, turn round so that I may see your new dress, your lumber-jacket lined with real sheepskin. Talk to me about the cinema, about painting. I'll read you the latest letter from the wives of small farmers, alone on their flat Normandy earth who struggle for their existence and that of their livestock ... before you go warm your cold little paws under my stuffed quilt.

Jean Cocteau comes in, and I look at him with amazement. It is half past eleven in the morning? If it were night I would not have been surprised. Anyway he replies before I ask the question:

'Yes – would you believe it, my camera-operators, my electricians, my carpenters, have just told me they're on strike.' He insinuates his long person onto the stern of my raft, folds his legs under him, crosses his arms, twists his body round, in such a way as to fit them into my beam of sunlight which marks the midday hour.

'Well?'

'Well nothing. I've left the studios.'

'Holiday! Have a rest. That's what one does.'

His nose looks sideways at me, perplexed. – 'No, that's just it – I can't any more. I have worked madly for years. Nights, days, Sundays, whatever I'm doing, at meals, at a restaurant table, out of doors in the country, on paper. Work used to annihilate, leave me for dead. Now I no longer know how to stop working, unless I know a long time ahead that I'll get a break. I'm off drugs again. My joints are stiff. It's a quarter to twelve. I'm not hungry yet. I'm never hungry. What does one *do* at a quarter to twelve when one's not working? I've forgotten.'

'Stay here.'

'I can't. One doesn't stay with you at a quarter to twelve.'

'Where do you want to go?'

'That's just it, I don't know. I shall try to go home.'

He says it in the tone of one embarking on a great new venture.

He uncurls himself. His angular grace disturbs nothing, displaces nothing on the littered bed, knocks against no obstacle in the narrow room. He is off. At the door he turns back: 'Watch me as I cross the gardens, I'm sure I shall walk sideways.'

Jean Marais and Yvonne de Bray rehearsed on her raft for the radio version of *Chéri*; a three-year-old boy from the flat below lugged his baby brother upstairs to show her; women wrote to her for advice on how to deal with their recalcitrant children; school-girls wrote under the impression that she was still at school, to tell her that they too were Claudines. But whilst absorbing the life that flowed towards her she still found time to write: between ten at night and three in the morning 'the indulgence of a writer relieved of telephone calls, friendly visits, and anyone's concern'.

L'Etoile Vesper was published in 1946. It is anecdotal, themeless, but full of riches:

When I was young I used to fiddle whilst writing. For instance, if I happened to hit upon the word 'murmur' and was groping for a continuation of my phrase, this was the moment to affix under each of the equal sections of the word a little caterpillar foot, one of those small sucker feet that cling so tenaciously to a branch. At one end of the word I would draw the rather equine head of the caterpillar, at the other end the terminal tail, a ravishing appendix. Instead of the word 'murmur' I now had the caterpillar symbol, much prettier. And I would remember Alphonse Allais, who, finding in the country one of those brown, opulent, velvety-haired caterpillars that are the marvels of their species, exclaimed: 'Look, a bear! But Lord, how small it is, how small.'

She had imagined that *L'Etoile Vesper* would be her last book, indeed the final line is: 'From here I can see the end of the road.' But there followed shorter works, the gathering together of earlier unpublished chronicles, and finally, in 1949, the marvellously robust *Le Fanal bleu.* Among the shorter works was *Pour un herbier*, twenty-two chapters on plants, flowers and herbs, for which Raoul Dufy did the watercolour illustrations. 'It is a great joy for me to collaborate in your "herbier",' he wrote to her, '... I am writing to you as I'm about to leave for the United States where I am hoping to find a cure for my rheumatism which has become intolerable.' In the same genre, *Flore et Pomone* had forty black-and-white illustrations by La Prade. From her unlikely raft in the heart of Paris she was still clinging to the earth and its fruits.

The Raft

OPPOSITE Marguerite Moreno as
Giraudoux's madwoman of Chaillot.
'Under the black and white plaster, under
the tawdry finery, a great artist.'
(*Le Fanal bleu*)

ON 14 JULY 1948 MARGUERITE MORENO'S NEPHEW, Pierre
Moreno, wrotc to tell Colette that Marguerite had died. She
had caught a chill while on tour, which had turned to pleurisy.
She died at the height of her powers and had just enjoyed a major
success in Giraudoux's *La Folle de Chaillot*. The deep affection
between Colette and Moreno had lasted more than fifty years.
When they could not visit each other, they telephoned; when they
were away from each other, they wrote.

In an article on her friend published in *Le Figaro littéraire* in
September of that year, Colette wrote:

I had the joy of applauding Moreno in *La Folle de Chaillot*. A sharp
attack of arthritis made me fear until the last moment that I would have to
stay at home. . . . I found at the Athénée exactly what I had anticipated:
the virtuosity, the verbosity of Giraudoux, and my own indifference. I
felt nothing at all for the text: it allowed me to devote myself to the décor
by the painter Bérard, to the irrepressible liking I have for Jouvet [the
director], to the total absolution for his arbitrary tyranny that I have to
accord him in repayment for his inventiveness. . . . And finally, I was able
to watch – I'm coming to it – only Marguerite Moreno, occupied in
creating under our eyes the role of La Folle. . . .

Though she sometimes played the very long role twice a day, she
still found time to visit Colette.

'You don't even look tired!'

'I am though. The stairs, the dry air which affects my throat ... and
standing so long on stage. . . .'

I interrupted her with a gesture she understood.

'Oh, yes, the tiringness of the part. . . . My Colette if I don't look very
tired its because I am not very tired. I am doing something which I don't
find very difficult. La Folle is a very long, eccentric part, but it has no
secrets. No psychological mystery, so it is not exhausting. Would you like
to know what I think? Who could I say this to, if not to you? I believe that
the part could be played by anybody.'

In 1949 Colette, at seventy-six, was unanimously elected President of the Académie Goncourt, succeeding after the death of Sacha

Guitry; and the following year she was presented with the Grande Médaille de la Ville de Paris.

But honours, no more than husbands, could do anything to change her free and earthy nature. Joyously, Yannick Bellon has caught on film Colette in her late seventies; a film she wrote and narrated which consists mostly of a camera's return to the many houses and gardens she had owned and loved. But at the beginning and the end of the film, Colette, propped up with cushions, is there in person, surrounded by her cases of butterflies, her paperweights and her marbles. At the opening she is breakfasting with Maurice, at the close she is visited by Cocteau. In contrast with the plump wrists and hands – short, mottled with the yellow-brown blemishes of old age, workman-like, thick-sct – the face has a beauty of great delicacy not caught in any of the photographs of her old age. It is a traditional mime's face beneath the grey fuzz of hair. The little pointed chin is feline; she has painted blue kohl all round her eyes, which has been her habit since her early music-hall days, and makes them shine in depth. She is delicately dressed in a silken negligée, and the atmosphere of frowsiness which surrounds old people long bed-ridden, has given way, for the cameras, to a newborn freshness. But the revelation is in the voice. It embodies what she is. It purrs, caresses the name of a fruit, the word *enfant* as if she had met them, pronounced them for the first time, and with joy. As the camera sweeps over a tanglewood of flowers she speaks their names with the thrill of a real, a scientific, discovery. Her voice has no angularities or stridencies; its earthy, grapey accent remains peasant, and through it can be heard the tone of her books, the ripe tone of lucid prose. She acts her everyday part with aplomb, but unemphatically, bites on an onion from the basket Pauline has brought back from the market, and seems to be tasting it with her tongue. Only the front of her mouth moves.

The scene is arranged, but not set; both she and Pauline ad lib a little ... then the voice caresses the earlier scenes of her life, and only returns to the red room towards the end of the film. In the meantime Georges Wague is interviewed. 'Yes,' he says, Colette had discipline and self-discipline, 'but she mimed and wrote like no-one else. I would suggest she dance something like so, "Yes, I'll do that," she replied, and she did something different. What she did was very personal to her.' They danced, he says, anywhere, in the lowest caf' conc' halls or in official theatres.

Back in the red room it is evident that Colette has also written an outline for a conversation with Cocteau. But he doesn't stick to it, instead he starts talking about her, the amount of work she still does, her tireless energy. She is embarrassed by the flattery, pushes it

'... paper-weights and sulphides which sparkled under the lights ... and were reflected in the looking-glass.' (Maurice Goudeket *Près de Colette*)

away with a plump little hand '*mais non, mais non*', as if she were not on solid ground and were imploring him mentally to stick to the script. But he does it delicately, and reveals that, in spite of all the honours bestowed on her, in spite of all her fame, she is still not totally sure of herself – vulnerable, easily unsettled.

As he leaves she puts her fingers against her mouth, kisses them lightly as a parting; her eyes reflect her femininity, betray that it is a man they are looking at. She picks up her tapestry at the end of the film as if to indicate that this had taken the place of writing. But she was mistaken. That same year she wrote *Le Fanal bleu* by the light of her bedside lamp around which was folded, as a shade, a funnel of the blue paper she had used for writing her novels ever since the long-ago days of writing for Willy in school exercise books.

'Sometimes I feel the need,' she wrote, 'sharp as thirst in summer, to know and to describe. And then I pick up my pen again and attempt the perilous and illusive task of seizing and pinning down under the flexible double-pointed nib, the many-hued fugitive thrilling adjective. The attack doesn't last long. It is but the itching of an old scar.' The itch was still with her at eighty, a year before her death: 'Are you there, my need to write? Are you really there, necessary, strong-limbed, emblematic, are you still there? I tap at your door, I sound out your presence. . . .'

Even to relinquish writing would not be as hard, she knew, as relinquishing the pleasure of thought, of recall, of living again and again in the places her memory treasured:

> 'Your leg isn't still hurting?'
> 'Not at all. I'm thinking.'
> I'm thinking. Can one really give the name of thoughts to a promenade, an aimless unplanned contemplation, a sort of virtuosity of memory that I'm not the only one to condemn as vain? I set off, I dash forward along a once familiar path, as fast as I used to pace, I see the great twisted oak, the poor farm where cider and bread and butter used to be generously doled out to me. Here is where the yellow road branches, the creamy white elders, surrounded by bees in such numbers that their threshing-machine hum can be heard at twenty paces. . . . I hear the sobbing of the guinea-fowl, the sow grumbling . . . that's the way I work . . . then, suddenly, a mental block, emptiness, annihilation, exactly resembling, or so I feel, what must be the approach to death, the road lost, barred, obliterated. . . .

At eighty she received the insignia of Grand Officier of the Légion d'honneur, the highest rank that any woman has attained, from the hands of the Minister of Education, André Marie. And the American Ambassador, Douglas Dillon, came to her bedside to offer her the diploma of the National Institute of Arts and Letters, in the presence of Prince Pierre of Monaco. But the world of honours and acclaim was not her real world. 'During those long years of physical pain,' wrote Bertrand de Jouvenel, 'you might see her on her couch sometimes with an apple or a shell in her hands, restoring to her the fullness of the orchard or the sea which she would never gaze upon any more. Her gentle and attentive last husband would comfort her with these humble messengers from her true land; they meant far more to her than any praise of her work.'

Though she never romanticised anything in nature, where her love of the apple or the shell differed from the scientist's was where the artist *must* differ. The scientist is intent not only on discovery, but on understanding in the sense of explaining, de-mystifying, the nature of a thing. Colette, whilst understanding, did not want to tamper with the essential mystery. To explain, to her, was to explain away. For a scientist to reach the moon and analyse a piece of it, to list its composition, is perhaps no nearer the heart of the matter than the artist who whilst noting its phases, does not wish to disturb its essential mooniness. Colette not only allowed, but wished, the moon to guard its mooniness, a fruit to keep the secret of its fruitiness, a shell its shellness. When she tasted, smelt, picked at a berry, she was entering into the life of the berry at the same time as making it a part of herself. Her senses, not a dispassionate mind, were involved. In a letter to Henri Mondor who had sent her a black lead drawing of a rose, she wrote: 'I am looking at it through my magnifying glass, and thank God, I can discover nothing, you have left it all its mystery.'

'... Sido, found again at last.' (Maurice Goudeket *Près de Colette*)

Two contrary movements marked the last years of her life [writes Maurice Goudeket]. The glow of fame which, swelling unceasingly, making its most resounding trumpets sound in her ears, multiplying honours for her, bringing to her table a pile of messages and to her door a flood of visitors, reached a summit rarely surpassed. And the slow ebb of Colette herself, who attempted to escape from the noise created around her, not from any disdain that she might have for it, but because, feeling her powers diminishing and incapable of giving things a less wondering attention, she fell back upon what was essential for her.... She took interest in fewer things, but not less in those. She rang for Pauline, asked her for a book of pictures representing plants, birds and insects. Nearly always now she used a magnifying glass, not because her sight had diminished but because she wanted to look more closely. And she asked to see her butterflies nearer ... the richly coloured butterflies which bounded her immediate horizon came from the Amazon.... Where the books lodged a narrow strip of wood enabled her to hang, in its contemporary frame, a little portrait of Sido at eighteen.... The chimney piece was covered, jammed, with paperweights and sulphides ... also in the flat were those Chinese crystal balls which satisfied Colette's two-fold taste for the limpidity of springs, and for circles. Glass walking-sticks, trum-

'... under the fur bedspread a hot-water bottle warmed her feet.' (Maurice Goudeket *Près de Colette*)

pets, pipes, and necklaces were hung and lodged all over the place.

Her writing, which had remained so firm, gradually changed, betraying the fatigue which she strove to hide.

The last page of her last book predicts this decline: 'With humility I shall write again, there is no other way for me. But when does one cease to write? What is the warning sign? A failure of the hand?'

In March 1954 she wrote to her friend Hélène Jourdain-Morhange, in a scarcely recognisable hand '... to show you that writing is yet another thing I must deprive myself of ... it is painful and I write to no-one ... a writer who can no longer write ... strange affliction. . . .'

A writer who can no longer write. Forty years earlier she had explained in *La Vagabonde* what writing meant to her:

To write, to be able to write, what does it mean? It means spending long hours dreaming before a white page, scribbling unconsciously, letting your pen play around a blot of ink and nibble at a half-formed word. . . . To write is to sit and stare, hypnotised, at the reflection of the window in the silver inkstand, to feel the divine fever mounting to one's cheeks and forehead while the hand that writes grows blissfully numb upon the paper. . . . To write is to pour one's innermost self passionately upon the tempting paper . . . and to find next day in place of the golden bough that bloomed so miraculously in that dazzling hour, a withered bramble and a stunted flower. Oh to write!

She had been in great pain for more than three years, endured it, worked in spite of it, kept an ever-vigilant interest in everything around her ... now the symptoms of decline became increasingly apparent:

Her memory detached itself from recent events so that it might better hold the deeply graven traces of the past. Two months before her end she found an old photograph taken at Saint-Sauveur school which shows her among thirty little girls. . . . She named them all, one after another, without hesitation.

Then came the day when she was too weak to raise herself. It was towards the twentieth of July. Colette de Jouvenel, Pauline and I started a vigil. . . .

The day before her death, Goudeket, watching her half-closed eyes, and her lips moving, believed she was holding a long discourse with Sido: that she was back again with her mother in the garden of her childhood.

She died at half past seven on the evening of 3 August 1954.

Colette is the only woman in France ever to have been given a state funeral.

Writers from all over the world came to pay their respects and to

'I'm surprised that I've changed; that I've grown old whilst I dreamed.' (*Les Vrilles de la vigne*) Minet-Chéri is fourth from the left in the front row.

show their love, and the people of France in their thousands filed past the coffin and the great mass of flower tributes in the gardens of the Palais-Royal, then the long cortège passed up the Champs-Elysées – with no priest in attendance. She was buried in the Père-Lachaise Cemetery, with no Christian rites, no cross upon her grave, no service in the Saint-Roch Church on the way.

Graham Greene, shocked to the depths of his being by the lack of Catholic ceremony, wrote an open letter to the Cardinal-Archbishop of Paris, Cardinal Feltin, which was printed next day on the front page of *Le Figaro littéraire*:

Eminence,

Those who love Colette and her works are united today to honour her in a ceremony which must have seemed to Catholics strangely truncated. We are used to praying for our dead. In our faith, the dead are never abandoned. It is the right of every person baptised a Catholic to be accompanied by a priest as far as the grave. We cannot lose this right – as one can lose the right of citizenship of a temporary country – by any crime or offence, for the reason that no human being is capable of judging another, nor of deciding where his faults commence, or his merits end. But today, by your decision, no priest has offered public prayers at the obsequies of Colette. Your reasons are known to us all. But would they have been invoked if Colette had been less illustrious? Forget the great writer and remember an old lady of eighty who at the time when your Eminence had not yet been ordained, made an unhappy marriage, not through her own fault (unless innocence be a fault) and afterwards broke the law of the Church by a second and a third civil marriage. Two civil marriages, are they so unpardonable? The life of some of our Saints offer us worse examples. Certainly they repented. But to repent signifies that one has reconsidered one's life, and no-one can say what passes in the souls of

223

those who see clearly when they are confronted by the imminent fact of death. You have condemned on insufficient evidence, because neither you nor any of your officiating priests was with her. Your Eminence has unknowingly given the impression that the Church pursues a transgression beyond the death-bed. For what purpose has Your Eminence set this example? Is it to warn your flock of the dangers of treating the laws of marriage lightly? It would certainly have been of more value to warn them of the dangers of condemning others too easily, and preserve them from lack of charity. Religious authorities frequently remind writers of their responsibility towards simple souls, and the risks of shocking them. But there exists also another risk, that of shocking souls which are aware. Has Your Eminence not considered that a shock of this nature might be caused by your decision? To non-Catholics it might seem that the Church itself is lacking in charity; that the Church itself can refuse its prayers at the moment of greatest need. How differently Gide was treated by the Protestant Church when he died! (Your Eminence will pardon the heat of these expressions in remembering that a writer whose books we love becomes for us a dearly loved person. This is not an abstract matter taken from a collection on moral theology for use in seminaries.) Of course, on reflection, Catholics might realise that the voice of an archbishop is not necessarily the voice of the Church; but many Catholics, not only in France, but in England and America, where the works of Colette are known and loved, will feel wounded by the fact that Your Eminence, from a too strict interpretation of the rule, seems to deny the hope of that final intervention of grace on which surely Your Eminence and all of us depend in our final hour.

With my humble respects for the Sacred Purple

Graham Greene

Paris 7 August 1954.

Neither death nor religion had preoccupied her during her life. The only clue to what ceremony she might have wished for herself was written as early as 1913, a newspaper piece on the cemetery in Montmartre:

... a dwarf city, maisonnettes, chapel-huts and mausoleum-hutches, all in massive stone, iron, marble, moulded, hewn in serene bad taste, with childish vanity which does not disarm, but instead provokes a shrug of the shoulders, an affronted laugh ... I am revolted by the idea of a licensed charnel house, permitted in the centre of the city on show between a new hotel and a cinema. A charnel-house ... when we have at our command, obedient, joyous, ready to leap, to destroy, to purify, to disperse the frightful remains of ourselves – we have Fire....

Chronology

1829   Birth of Jules-Joseph Colette

1835   Birth of Adèle-Eugénie-Sidonie Landoy (Sido)

1857   Marriage of Sido and Jules Robineau-Duclos

1860   Birth of Juliette Robineau-Duclos

1863   Birth of Achille Robineau-Duclos

1865   January: Death of Jules Robineau-Duclos
        December: Marriage of Sido and Captain Jules-Joseph Colette

1868   Birth of Léopold Colette (Léo)

1873   28 January: Birth of Sidonie-Gabrielle Colette (Colette) in
        Saint-Sauveur-en-Puisaye

1893   15 May: Marriage of Colette and Henry Gauthier-Villars (Willy)

1900   *Claudine à l'école*, signed by Willy

1901   *Claudine à Paris*, signed by Willy

1902   *Claudine en ménage*, signed by Willy
        22 January: 'Claudine à Paris' play-adaptation, opens at
        the Théâtre des Bouffes-Parisiens

1903   *Claudine s'en va*, signed by Willy

1904   *Minne*, signed by Willy
        Dialogues de bêtes, for the first time signed by Colette:
        Colette Willy

1905   *Les Egarements de Minne*, signed by Willy
        Sept dialogues de bêtes Colette Willy
        Death of Jules-Joseph Colette

1906   Colette and Willy separate
        6 February: Colette dances on stage for the first time in the
        mime-drama 'Le Désir, l'amour et la chimère at the
        Théâtre des Mathurias
        1 October: Mime-drama 'La Romanichelle' at l'Olympia
        28 November: Mime-drama 'Pan' at the Théâtre Marigny

1907   *La Retraite sentimentale* Colette Willy
        3 January: The mime-drama 'Rêve d'Egypte' at the Moulin-
        Rouge provokes a scandal

27 April: Serialisation of *Les Vrìlles de la vigne* begins in *La Vie parisienne*

2 November: Mime-drama 'La Chair' at l'Apollo

1908 *Les Vrìlles de la vigne* published

Colette goes on tour as Claudine in 'Claudine à Paris'

1909 *L'Ingénue libertine* published

February: Two-act play 'En camarades' at the Théâtre des Arts, written and acted by Colette Willy

April–June: Tour of the Midi in 'Claudine à Paris' and 'La Chair'

1910 May: Serialisation of *La Vagabonde* begins in *La Vie parisienne*

June: Divorce of Colette and Henry Gauthier-Villars

December: Colette begins journalistic work for *Le Matin*

1911 *La Vagabonde* published

1912 September: Death of Sido

December: Marriage of Colette and Henry de Jouvenel

1913 *L'Entrave*

L'Envers du music-hall

Prrou, Poucette et quelques autres

3 July: Birth of Colette de Jouvenel

1914 2 August: Henry de Jouvenel mobilised

December: Colette in Verdun

1915 Journey to Rome and Venice

1917 *Les Heures longues*

1919 *Mitsou*

Colette becomes literary editor of *Le Matin*

1920 *Chéri* serialised and published

September: Colette becomes Chevalier de la Légion d'honneur

1921 December: 'Chéri' opens at the Théâtre Michel

1922 *La Maison de Claudine*

28 February: Colette plays Lea for the 100th performance of 'Chéri'

April: *Le Blé en herbe* is serialised in *Le Matin*

1923 *Le Blé en herbe* – for the first time under the signature Colette

February: 'La Vagabonde' opens at the Théâtre de la Renaissance

December: Colette and Henry de Jouvenel separate

1925 21 March: 'L'Enfant et les sortilèges', libretto by Colette, music by Maurice Ravel, opens in Monte Carlo

April: Colette meets Maurice Goudeket

1926 *La Fin de Chéri*

1 February: 'L'Enfant et les sortilèges' opens in Paris at the Opéra-Comique

Colette buys La Treille muscate at St Tropez

1928 *La Naissance du jour*

November: Colette promoted to Officier de la Légion d'honneur

1929 *La Seconde*
1930 *Sido*
1931 January: Death of Willy
September: Colette fractures her hip
December: Serialisation of *Ces Plaisirs . . .* (*Le Pur et l'impur*) begins in *Gringoire*
1932 *Prisons et paradis*
Ces Plaisirs . . .
1 June: Colette opens her beauty salon in Paris
1933 *La Chatte*
1934 *Duo*
1st volume of *La Jumelle noire* (theatre criticisms)
1935 2nd volume of *La Jumelle noire*
3 April: Marriage of Colette and Maurice Goudeket
June: Journey to New York on maiden voyage of the *Normandie*
October: Death of Henry de Jouvenel
1936 *Mes apprentissages*
February: Colette is promoted to Commandeur de la Légion d'honneur
1937 3rd volume of *La Jumelle noire*
1938 4th volume of *La Jumelle noire*
1939 *Le Toutounnier*
1940 *Chambre d'hôtel*
March: Death of Léo
1941 *Journal à rebours*
Julie de Carneilhan
12 December: Maurice Goudeket arrested by the Germans
1942 Maurice Goudeket freed
1943 *Le Képi*
Flore et Pomone
1944 *Gigi*
Trois . . . six . . . neuf
1945 *Belles Saisons*
May: Colette is elected to the Académie Goncourt
1946 *L'Etoile Vesper*
1948 *Pour un herbier*
1949 *Le Fanal bleu*
October: Colette elected president of the Académie Goncourt
1951 Film, *Colette*, directed by Yannich Bellon
1953 Colette becomes Grand Officier de la Légion d'honneur
1954 3 August: Death of Colette
7 August: State funeral

Notes

Where the translations are not credited to anyone else they are by the author.
Where the source appears in the text it is not requoted in the notes.

1 Childhood

p 10 'They say that children ...' *La Maison de Claudine*

'To lay bare ...' *Sido*

'dim by writing ...' *Journal à rebours*

p 11 'the purr-purr as of a log fire ...' *La Maison de Claudine*

p 12 'imprints like flowers ...' *La Maison de Claudine* tr. *My Mother's House* Una Vincenzo Troubridge and Enid McLeod

p 18 'Sido laughed ...' *Sido*

'ennobled with paganism ...' *Les Vrilles de la vigne*

'I inhabited a paradise ...' Ibid

p 19 'Be quiet ...' *Sido*

'My moss roses ...' Ibid

'no more to be revered ...' *La Naissance du jour*

'You see they had never ...' *Journal à rebours*

p 20 'Just think ...' *Sido*

'Madame Thorazeau ...' *En pays connu*

p 21 'press upon her own ...' *My Mother's House* tr. Troubridge and McLeod

'Minet – Chéri, come and see ...' *La Maison de Claudine*

p 22 'Shows imagination ...' *Journal à rebours*

p 24 'To My Dear Soul ...' *Sido*

'Poor Moffino ...' *En pays connu*

'Go on, UP ...' *Sido*

p 25 'Good memory ...' *Mes apprentissages*

p 27 'bringing books ...' Noces (Oeuvres complètes Vol VII Flammarion)

p 30 'She looks a bit like ...' Ibid

'Next day ...' Ibid

2 Willy

p 32 'glorifying ribboned knickers ...' *Mes apprentissages*

'M. Willy was not huge ...' *Mes apprentissages* tr. *My Apprenticeships* Helen Beauclerk

p 34 'secret certainty of being ...' *Les Vrilles de la vigne*

p 35 'a thin, thin Colette ...' Jean Cocteau in *Portraits Souvenir* tr. *Paris Album* Margaret Crosland

p 36 'Proust came one evening ...' *Belles Saisons*

p 37 'Yes, yes, and the cellos ...' *En pays connu*

'He had a distant ...' *Journal à rebours*

'I knew the yellow ...' Jean Cocteau in *Paris Album* tr. Crosland

p 37 'laborious, exhausting ...' *My Apprenticeships* tr. Beauclerk
'I was just as miserable ...' *Le Pur et l'impur*
p 38 'no sooner married ...' *Mes apprentissages*
p 41 'leered like an evil-minded ...' Ibid
'the conditions of my life ...' *My Apprenticeships* tr. Beauclerk
p 45 'the end of my character ...' Ibid
'one day it occurred ...' Ibid
p 47 'Don't be afraid ...' *Mes apprentissages*
p 48 'I was mistaken ...' Ibid
'Fancy, I thought ...' Ibid
p 50 'an expression ...' Ibid
'Intimidated by Forain ...' *Paris de ma fenêtre*
'Black fire, a red crater ...' *Prisons et paradis*
p 52 'voluble, white ...' *Mes apprentissages*
'You're the author ...' Ibid
p 53 'the sound of the key ...' *My apprenticeships* tr. Beauclerk

3 Claudine

p 58 'Her flat-topped ...' Jean Cocteau in *Portraits-Souvenir* tr. *Paris Album* – Margaret Crosland
p 61 'Monsieur Willy has created ...' Georges Casella in *La Revue Dorée*
'Claudine, enigmatic ...' Joseph Montet in *Tout Paris*
'that immortal Claudine ...' Camille Pert in *L'Information des gens de Lettres*
'She is adorably scandalous ...' Paul André
'I would not give ...' Paul Bernard in *L'Opinion* (Saigon)
'... her favourite companions ...' Natalie Clifford Barney in *Souvenirs indiscrets*
'faithful to their concept ...' *Le Pur et l'impur* tr. *The Pure and the Impure* Herma Briffault
p 67 'to save up crumbs ...' *Mes apprentissages* tr. *My Apprenticeships* Helen Beauclerk
p 72 'Was it love ...' *Mes apprentissages*
p 73 'If you would like ...' Ibid

4 Missy

p 76 'I am so made ...' *Mes apprentissages* tr. *My Apprenticeships* Helen Beauclerk
'such as you know ...' *Mes apprentissages*
'If the novel ...' Ibid
p 77 'Who's barking ...' *Les Vrilles de la vigne*
p 78 'He was given the handsomest ...' *La Maison de Claudine* tr. *My Mother's House* Una Vincenzo Troubridge and Enid McLeod
p 80 'I am the Marquise ...' Sylvain Bonmariage in *Willy, Colette et moi*
p 81 'laborious, sexual ...' *My Apprenticeships* tr. Beauclerk
'The shadow ...' *Le Pur et l'impur* tr. *The Pure and the Impure* Herma Briffault
p 82 'Since Proust ...' Ibid
'demons of fever ...' *Les Vrilles de la vigne*
'At the back ...' *La Maison de Claudine*
p 86 'Very quickly ...' *La Vagabonde* tr. *The Vagabond* Enid McLeod
'... she gives at the same time ...' Louis Delluc in *Comoedia Illustré*
'She lacked even ...' André Rouveyre

'... characteristic of Colette ...' *L'Album Comique*
'She emitted an indefinable ...' Sylvain Bonmariage in *Willy, Colette et moi*
p 86 'How marvellously ...' Ibid
p 91 'monstrous simplicity ...' *La Naissance du jour*

5 La Vagabonde

p 96 'Maudes, the Lianes ...' *Mes apprentissages*
p 100 'Ninety-six in the shade, eh ...' *L'Envers du music-hall* tr. *Music-hall Sidelights* Ann-Marie Callimachi
p 102 'How long had it ...' *La Vagabonde* tr. *The Vagabond* Enid McLeod
'A phrase of music ...' *Mes apprentissages*
p 104 'I move my head imperceptibly ...' *The Vagabond* tr. McLeod
p 105 'The language spoken ...' 'Les bêtes avant tout, surtout,/Parlent le language des bêtes,
Que nous ne savons pas du tout/Et que seule comprend Colette'
'Ouf! Je métouffe ...' Notes for *Prisons et paradis*
'Help! I've been locked ...' *Trois ... six ... neuf*
'At last, there you are ...' *Les Vrilles de la vigne*
p 106 'Here is zummer ...' 'Foissi l'été, elle est bien chaute,/Et le soleil prille comme une crosse hétoile,
Et la lune elle nous s'éclaire/Pentant toute la nuit'
'for my part ...' *Paysages et portraits*

6 Sidi

p 112 'To have had the chance ...' in *L'Epoque contemporaine* 1905–1930
p 113 'groomed, polished ...' *L'Etoile Vesper* tr. *The Evening Star* David le Vay
'When I come into a room ...' *La Naissance du jour*
p 114 'as tall as three apples ...' *L'Etoile Vesper*
p 116 'Three hundred feet ...' *Contes des mille et un matins*
'There's something over there ...' Ibid
p 118 'Ah! I'm not happy ...' *La Naissance du jour*
p 119 'A small hand ...' *Contes des mille et un matins*
p 121 'Princess Marthe ...' Renaud de Jouvenel: notes to the author
'The façade was eroded ...' Ibid
'Sido – to whom I wrote ...' *Mes apprentissages*
p 124 'Don't let me ever ...' *La Maison de Claudine* tr. *My Mother's House* Una Vincenzo
Troubridge and Enid McLeod
'... bitches, their pups ...' *En pays connu*
p 125 '*La Vie parisienne* which was ...' *L'Etoile Vesper* tr. *The Evening Star* David Le Vay
'Euphoria, purring ...' Ibid
'Her nails, resembling ...' Ibid
p 126 'I shall sit outside ...' *La Chambre éclairée*
p 128 'I leaned out ...' *Le Fanal bleu*
Annie de Pène: journalist on *Le Matin*.
Musidora: actress who later played in a film of *La Vagabonde*.

7 War

p 134 'Venice has kept ...' *Contes des mille et un matins*

p 134 '... a second round ...' Ibid

'... the most sickening task' Letter to Georges Wague

p 135 'when I met him again' *Belles Saisons*

'A snapshot ...' *L'Etoile Vesper* tr. *The Evening Star* David Le Vay

p 136 'Aunt Colette ...' *La Revue de Paris* 1966

'If you would know ...' *Time and Tide* 1954

p 138 'I had a strange ...' Renaud de Jouvenel in *La Revue de Paris* 1966

p 139 'She certainly loved ...' Renaud de Jouvenel: notes to the author

'A proud look ...' Ibid

'She exaggerated ...' Renaud de Jouvenel *La Revue de Paris* 1966

p 140 'Can't you write ...' *La Naissance du jour*

p 143 'If he hadn't been ...' Ibid

'Chéri? He was ...' Preface to *Chéri* (Flammarion)

'He wants everything ...' Ibid

p 144 'You do exist then ...' Ibid

'I shall no doubt ...' *The Evening Star* tr. David Le Vay

p 146 'How pleased she seemed ...' *Nouvelles Littéraires* 1924

'I overthrew the idols ...' Colette in *Journal de Monaco* 1924

p 147 'No-one can replace her ...' *Fantasia*

'Don't let Madame ...' André Rouveyre in *Mercure de France* 1926

'... she does not act ...' Gerard d'Houville (Marie de Régnier) in *Mercure de France* 1925

p 152 'Did she play a part ...' Renaud de Jouvenel: notes to the author

p 153 'I speak on stages ...' Letter to Marguerite Moreno

p 154 'people believed ...' Renaud de Jouvenel: interview with the author

8 Paradise Regained

p 158 '... as I entered ...' Maurice Goudeket in *Près de Colette*

'I thought that evening ...' Maurice Goudeket interview with the author

p 159 'My infatuation ...' Maurice Goudeket *Près de Colette*

'I had never learned ...' Ibid

'I found it ...' *Prisons et paradis*

p 162 'I will tell you ...' *Paysages et portraits*

'Armed only with ...' *Claudine s'en va*

'With Colette ...' Maurice Goudeket in *Près de Colette*

p 163 'Is this my last ...' *La Naissance du jour*

p 168 'nasty old witch ...' Renaud de Jouvenel: letter to the author

'I want to be Jewish ...' Colette de Jouvenel: interview with the author

p 174 'protected from the whole ...' *La Vagabonde* tr. *The Vagabond* Enid McLeod

9 Remembrance of Things Past

p 183 'You think she's ...' *Dialogues de bêtes*

'I haven't the heart ...' *Le Fanal bleu*

'You don't look well ...' Maurice Goudeket in *Près de Colette*

p 185 'I still ask myself ...' *Paysages et portraits*

p 189 'a fine talent ...' *La Gazette de Paris*

'... a masterpiece ...' Edmond Jaloux in *L'Excelsior*

p 190 'a duet between ...' Margaret Davies in *Colette*

p 191 'I thought he was ...' Renaud de Jouvenel: interview with the author

'If we had not ...' Maurice Goudeket in *Près de Colette*

'Conjure up a cat ...' Ibid

p 194 'Don't stand there suffering ...' Colette de Jouvenel reported by Virginia Lee Warren *N Y Times* 1970

'You'd think by ...' Renaud de Jouvenel: interview with the author

p 198 'She was as ...' *Prisons et paradis*

'Now I possess ...' *Le Fanal bleu*

10 The Occupation

p 200 'since it is now ...' Colette: Radio Paris-Mondial

'two medieval castles ...' Maurice Goudeket in *Près de Colette*

'I'm used to spending ...' Ibid

p 202 'You, Jewess ...' Ibid

'humbly among those ...' *L'Etoile Vesper* tr. *The Evening Star* David Le Vay

'What "resistance" ...' Ibid

p 203 'to wait in Paris ...' Ibid

'Once they had gone ...' Ibid

'I may not always ...' Ibid

p 205 'the cries and appeals ...' Ibid

'I don't think you quite ...' Maurice Goudeket in *Près de Colette*

p 208 'Like the other districts ...' *The Evening Star* tr. David Le Vay

'He would make his way ...' Ibid

'We were still in the ...' Ibid

p 209 'The worst for an arthritic ...' *Le Fanal bleu*

p 210 'Aspirin ...' Maurice Goudeket in *Près de Colette*

p 211 'Come in ...' *The Evening Star* tr. David Le Vay

'Jean Cocteau ...' *Le Fanal bleu*

p 212 'the indulgence of a ...' *The Evening Star* tr. David Le Vay

11 The Raft

p 214 'You don't even ...' *Le Fanal bleu*

p 218 'Sometimes I feel the need ...' *La Vagabonde* tr. *The Vagabond* Enid McLeod

'Are you there ...' *Belles Saisons*

'Your leg isn't ...' *L'Etoile Vesper* tr. *The Evening Star* David Le Vay

p 219 'During those long ...' *Time and Tide* 1954

'Two contrary movements ...' Maurice Goudeket in *Près de Colette*

p 222 'With humility ...' *Le Fanal bleu*

'Her memory ...' Maurice Goudeket in *Près de Colette*

p 224 'a dwarf city ...' *Contes des mille et un matins*

Bibliography

The Principal Works of Colette
Novels
Le Blé en herbe Flammarion 1923; *Ripening Seed* Secker & Warburg
La Chatte Grasset 1933; *The Cat* Secker & Warburg 1953; *7 by
Colette* Farrar, Strauss & Cudahy 1955
Chéri A. Fayard 1920; *Chéri & The Last of Chéri* Secker & Warburg
1951; Farrar, Strauss & Young 1953
Claudine à l'école Ollendorf 1900; *Claudine at School* Secker &
Warburg 1956; Farrar, Strauss & Cudahy 1957
Claudine à Paris Ollendorf 1901; *Claudine in Paris* Farrar, Strauss &
Cudahy 1958
Claudine en ménage Ollendorf 1902; *The Indulgent Husband* Rinehart
1935; *Claudine Married* Secker & Warburg 1960
Claudine s'en va Ollendorf 1903; *The Innocent Wife* Farrar & Rinehart
1934

NOTE: The four *Claudines* were attributed to Willy until 1906;
from 1906–1948 to Willy and Colette Willy; from 1949–1955
(*Oeuvres complètes*) to Colette; since 1955, to Willy and Colette.

Dialogues de bêtes Mercure de France 1904; *Creatures Great and Small*
Secker & Warburg 1951; Farrar, Strauss & Cudahy 1957
Duo J. Ferenczi et Fils 1934; *The Married Lover* Werner Laurie 1935;
Duo Farrar & Rinehart 1935
L'Entrave Librairie des Lettres 1913; *Recaptured* Gollancz 1931;
Cosmopolitan Book Corporation 1931
La Fin de Chéri Flammarion 1926; see *Chéri*
Gigi La Guilde du livre, Lausanne; *Gigi* Farrar, Strauss & Cudahy 1959
L'Ingénue libertine Ollendorf 1909; *The Gentle Libertine* Farrar &
Rinehart 1931
Julie de Carneilhan A. Fayard 1941; *Julie de Carneilhan* Secker &
Warburg 1952; Farrar Strauss & Cudahy 1952
Le Képi A. Fayard 1943; In *The Tender Shoot & Other Stories* Farrar,
Strauss and Cudahy 1959
La Naissance du jour Flammarion 1928; *Morning Glory* Gollancz 1932
La Retraite Sentimentale Mecure de France 1907; *The Retreat from
Love* Peter Owen 1973
La Vagabonde Ollendorf 1911; *The Vagabond* Secker & Warburg 1954;
Farrar, Strauss & Young 1955
Les Vrilles de la vigne published by *La Vie parisienne* 1908

Autobiographical and Other Works
Belles Saisons Galerie Charpentres 1945
Contes des mille et un matins Flammarion 1970; *The Thousand & One Mornings* Peter Owen 1973 (Newspaper chronicles published in *Le Matin*)
En pays connu Bruker 1949
L'Envers du music-hall Flammarion 1913; *Music-hall Sidelights* Farrar, Strauss & Cudahy 1958
L'Etoile Vesper Milieu du Monde, Geneva 1946; *The Evening Star* Peter Owen 1973
Le Fanal bleu Ferenczi 1949
Les Heures longues A. Fayard 1917 (collection of war reports)
Journal à rebours A. Fayard 1941
La Jumelle noire Ferenczi 1934–38 (theatre reviews)
La Maison de Claudine Ferenczi 1922; *The Mother of Claudine* Werner Laurie 1937; *My Mother's House* Secker & Warburg 1953; Farrar, Strauss & Young 1953
Mes apprentissages Ferenczi 1936; *My Apprenticeships* Secker & Warburg 1957
Pour un herbier Mermod, Lausanne 1951
Prisons et paradis Ferenczi 1932
Le Pur et l'impur (Ces Plaisirs ...) Ferenczi 1932; *The Pure and The Impure* Secker & Warburg 1968
Sido Ferenczi 1930; *Sido* Secker & Warburg 1953
Trois ... six ... neuf Correa 1944
Le Voyage égoiste Edouard Pelletan 1922; *Journey for Myself* Peter Owen 1973

NOTE: In 1950 Flammarion published in 15 volumes the *Oeuvres complètes* of Colette. In 1973 Le Club de l'honnête homme published a centenary edition in 16 illustrated volumes of *Les Oeuvres complètes.*

Letters
Lettres a Marguerite Moreno Flammarion 1959
Lettres a ses paires Flammarion 1973
Lettres de la Vagabonde Flammarion 1961

Collections
Phelps, Robert *Earthly Paradise* (writings chosen from Colette's works) Farrar, Strauss & Giroux 1966

Other Sources
Barney, Natalie Clifford *Souvenirs indiscrets* Flammarion 1960
Bonmariage, Sylvain *Willy, Colette et moi* Frémanger 1954; Froissart 1954
Chauvière, Claude *Colette* Firmin-Didot 1931
Goudeket, Maurice *Près de Colette* Flammarion 1956; tr. *Close to Colette* Farrar, Strauss & Cudahy 1957
La Hire, Jean de *Ménages d'artistes* Adolphe d'Espie 1905

Acknowledgments

The author and publishers wish to thank: M. Renaud de Jouvenel for his letters and tape-recording, and for the use of photographs from his family album; Mme Monique Cornand, Mlle Madeleine Barbin and Mlle Marie-Laure Chastang of the Bibliothèque Nationale for their invaluable research for the Colette exhibition of 1973; Mlle Evèzard of the Société des Amis de Colette; Mlle Anne Berthoud of the Institut Français; with special thanks to James Bramwell.

Photographs are reproduced by the permission of: Agence de Presse Bernard 215; Bibliothèque Nationale 16–17, 23 (Mme Florence Gould), 28–9 (Mme Colette de Jouvenel), 31, 57, 60, 65, 67, 75, 84 (Mme Florence Gould), 87, 89, 95, 114, 115, 117, 120 (Maître Louis Guitard et Mme Ginette Guitard Auviste), 131, 142, 157, 165, 175, 182, 192–3, 197, 212, 217, 219, 223; Bulloz 42–3; Collection Brisgand 55; René Dazy 39, 62, 99, 148–9, 166, 188, 190; Giraudon 129; John Hillelson Agency 213 (photo Henri Cartier-Bresson); M. Renaud de Jouvenel 111, 122–3, 126, 127, 138, 194 (photo Renaud de Jouvenel); MAS, Barcelona 51; Popperfoto 201, 209; Radio Times Hulton Picture Library 199; Roger Viollet 9, 11, 12, 14, 79, 80, 83, 90, 133, 181, 206–7, 220–21; Georges Sirot 27, 171; Studio Martina-Latour 25, 41, 68–9, 97, 103, 108, 137, 141, 164, 167, 169; Société des Amis de Colette 47, 92 (Maurice Couture), 179 (photo Leinens), 210; Weidenfeld and Nicolson Archives 196.

Index

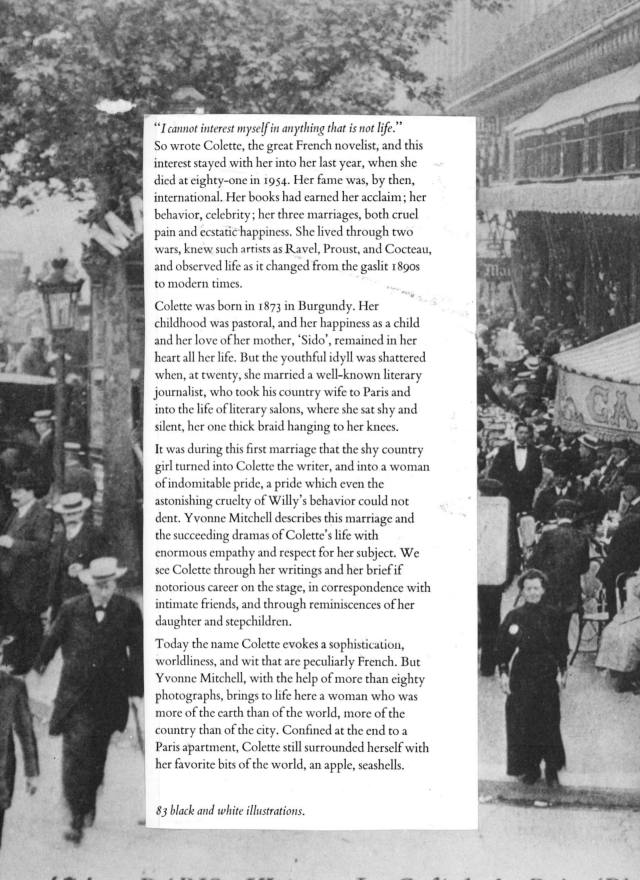

"*I cannot interest myself in anything that is not life.*"
So wrote Colette, the great French novelist, and this
interest stayed with her into her last year, when she
died at eighty-one in 1954. Her fame was, by then,
international. Her books had earned her acclaim; her
behavior, celebrity; her three marriages, both cruel
pain and ecstatic happiness. She lived through two
wars, knew such artists as Ravel, Proust, and Cocteau,
and observed life as it changed from the gaslit 1890s
to modern times.

Colette was born in 1873 in Burgundy. Her
childhood was pastoral, and her happiness as a child
and her love of her mother, 'Sido', remained in her
heart all her life. But the youthful idyll was shattered
when, at twenty, she married a well-known literary
journalist, who took his country wife to Paris and
into the life of literary salons, where she sat shy and
silent, her one thick braid hanging to her knees.

It was during this first marriage that the shy country
girl turned into Colette the writer, and into a woman
of indomitable pride, a pride which even the
astonishing cruelty of Willy's behavior could not
dent. Yvonne Mitchell describes this marriage and
the succeeding dramas of Colette's life with
enormous empathy and respect for her subject. We
see Colette through her writings and her brief if
notorious career on the stage, in correspondence with
intimate friends, and through reminiscences of her
daughter and stepchildren.

Today the name Colette evokes a sophistication,
worldliness, and wit that are peculiarly French. But
Yvonne Mitchell, with the help of more than eighty
photographs, brings to life here a woman who was
more of the earth than of the world, more of the
country than of the city. Confined at the end to a
Paris apartment, Colette still surrounded herself with
her favorite bits of the world, an apple, seashells.

83 black and white illustrations.